The Shakes

THE SHAKESPEARE HANDBOOKS

Series Editor: John Russell Brown

PUBLISHED

John Russell Brown	*Hamlet*
John Russell Brown	*Macbeth*
Paul Edmondson	*Twelfth Night*
Bridget Escolme	*Antony and Cleopatra*
Kevin Ewert	*Henry V*
Margaret Jane Kidnie	*The Taming of the Shrew*
Christopher McCullough	*The Merchant of Venice*
Paul Prescott	*Richard III*
Lesley Wade Soule	*As You Like It*

FORTHCOMING

Roger Apfelbaum	*Much Ado About Nothing*
David Carnegie	*Julius Caesar*
Trevor Griffiths	*The Tempest*
Stuart Hampton-Reeves	*Measure for Measure*
Edward L. Rocklin	*Romeo and Juliet*
Martin White	*A Midsummer Night's Dream*

The Shakespeare Handbooks

Hamlet

John Russell Brown

palgrave
macmillan

First published 2006 by
PALGRAVE MACMILLAN
Houndmills, Basingstoke, Hampshire, RG21 6XS and
175 Fifth Avenue, New York, N.Y. 10010
Companies and representatives throughout the world

PALGRAVE MACMILLAN is the global academic imprint of the
Palgrave Macmillan division of St. Martin's Press, LLC and of
Palgrave Macmillan Ltd. Macmillan® is a registered trademark in
the United States, United Kingdom and other countries. Palgrave is
a registered trademark in the European Union and other countries.

ISBN-13: 978–1–4039–3387–4 hardback
ISBN-10: 1–4039–3387–1   hardback
ISBN-13: 978–1–4039–2092–8 paperback
ISBN-10: 1–4039–2092–3   paperback

This book is printed on paper suitable for recycling and made
from fully managed and sustained forest sources.

A catalogue record for this book is available from the
British Library.

A catalog record for this book is available from the
Library of Congress

10	9	8	7	6	5	4	3	2	1
15	14	13	12	11	10	09	08	07	06

Printed in China

Contents

General Editor's Preface   vi

Preface   vii

1   The Texts and Early Performances   1

2   The Play's Sources and Cultural Context   12

3   Commentary   31

4   Key Productions and Performances   133

5   The Play on Screen   155

6   Critical Assessments   160

Further Reading   170

Index   176

General Editor's Preface

The Shakespeare Handbooks provide an innovative way of studying the theatrical life of the plays. The commentaries, which are their core feature, enable a reader to envisage the words of a text unfurling in performance, involving actions and meanings not readily perceived except in rehearsal or performance. The aim is to present the plays in the environment for which they were written and to offer an experience as close as possible to an audience's progressive experience of a production.

While each book has the same range of contents, their authors have been encouraged to shape them according to their own critical and scholarly understanding and their first-hand experience of theatre practice. The various chapters are designed to complement the commentaries: the cultural context of each play is presented together with quotations from original sources; the authority of its text or texts is considered with what is known of the earliest performances; key performances and productions of its subsequent stage history are both described and compared. The aim in all this has been to help readers to develop their own informed and imaginative view of a play in ways that supplement the provision of standard editions and are more user-friendly than detailed stage histories or collections of criticism from diverse sources.

Further volumes are in preparation so that, within a few years, the Shakespeare Handbooks will be available for all the plays that are frequently performed and studied.

John Russell Brown

Preface

The Tragedy of Hamlet, being one of the longest of Shakespeare's plays and having three early editions of very different authority, has called for a correspondingly lengthy commentary. In view of the subtlety and richness of its dialogue and its openness to many interpretations, the space allotted for this chapter in other volumes of this series would have been insufficient without skimping and failing to share with the reader a sense of the play in performance. Nor could some crucial textual problems be considered in the context of performance. This has meant that other chapters are shorter than usual, the brunt of these economies being borne by Chapter 6, on 'Critical Assessments'. The sheer number of writings on *Hamlet* would have made a comprehensive account another very lengthy chapter, especially if each sample of criticism were to be placed in its context. Instead of quoting at length from leading critics, a selection of their salient judgements is therefore offered with a view to suggesting ideas to readers who have the commentary at hand and, by this means, helping them to form their own opinions. The brief samples of criticism are arranged under a number of headings designed to facilitate connections with a reading of the text and commentary.

The rest of this Handbook follows the pattern of other volumes except that the chapter on 'Sources and Context' is placed before, rather than after, the commentary. Shakespeare's possible sources for this play are not so extensive that they are most usefully read after the play, and the text is of its own time in so many ways that a reader will be better served by encountering some samples of contextual material before, rather than after, the play itself.

This book owes a great deal to the actors of New Fortune Theatre with whom I have worked on this play and to students and colleagues of the graduate Directing Course at Middlesex University; I am most grateful for such an open and enlightening engagement with the text. It has also benefited from my two-way discussions, as General Editor, with other Handbook authors: I am grateful for this community of interest, from which I have learned new ways of bringing the plays theatrically alive to readers of the texts.

In my research, I have much cause to be grateful to Sarah Jardine-Willoughby at Middlesex University Library, Sue Brock at the Shakespeare Centre, Stratford-upon-Avon, Nicky Rathbone at Birmingham Central Library, and Tom Dale Keever at Columbia University, New York. Coming last but by no means least, at Palgrave Macmillan Kate Wallis, my editor, together with Sonya Barker and Felicity Noble, could not have been more patient and helpful as the book was planned and takes its place alongside other Handbooks. And, furthermore, my book will have reached print in good order under the watchful eyes of Valery Rose and Jocelyn Stockley; I am once more greatly indebted to them. I am fortunate in having such assistance, and most grateful to them all.

Chapter 4 on 'Key Productions and Performances' draws upon a series of articles on 'Landmark Productions', published in *Around the Globe*, by the new Globe Theatre, especially on 'Shakespeare for the Sixties' (Autumn, 2004); I am much indebted to the stimulus provided by this commission. The Penguin edition, edited by T. J. B. Spencer (1980, many times reprinted, and brought up to date in 2005), is the source for all quotations and references to *Hamlet*, except where otherwise noted. Quotations and references to other Shakespeare plays are from the Oxford and Norton editions of 1988 and later.

John Russell Brown

1 *The Texts and Early Performances*

No single authoritative text of Shakespeare's *Tragedy of Hamlet, Prince of Denmark* is available to us. In the early years of the sixteenth century, the play was printed three times from three different and, to some extent, independent manuscripts and what is now known about these publications must be the starting place for any attempt to discover what Shakespeare had in mind as he wrote. That task is enormously difficult, first because there are many variants between the texts, and because it quickly becomes apparent that some of the smallest differences will affect performance. A choice between numerous possibilities will often depend upon an imaginative response to the whole play as well as knowledge of many typographical and bibliographical details. The pursuit of Shakespeare's *Hamlet* will always be adventurous and uncertain, even as its verbal brilliance, psychological insights, physical vitality and masterly storytelling engage our attention immediately. Although modern editions have been prepared with reference to all three early versions, readers should realize that there is no one and only record of what Shakespeare intended for performance.

The two early Quarto editions

According to its title page, 'The Tragical History of Hamlet, Prince of Denmark by William Shakespeare' was on sale in London bookshops in 1603 and had been printed 'for N.L.' (the initials of Nicholas Ling). This is now known as the First Quarto, or Q1, because it was made up of sheets of paper folded twice so that each sheet gave four leaves of paper that would become eight pages of type. Only two copies of this book are known to have survived, both slightly imperfect but together giving one complete text. The title page also tells us that this edition represents the play 'as it hath been diverse times acted by his Highness Servants in the City of London, as also in the two universities of Cambridge and Oxford, and elsewhere'. Because the former Chamberlain's Company had become the King's Men on 19 May 1603, after the accession of James I, this edition must have been on sale sometime after that date. And because the play is said to have been on tour, which usually happened in the summer months when theatres were closed for fear of the plague, publication must have been later that year.

So much seems clear enough, but on 26 July of the previous year, the manuscript of 'A book called the Revenge of Hamlet, Prince [of] Denmark, as it was lately acted by the Lord Chamberlain his Servants' had already been entered by James Roberts in the Stationer's Register, the official ledger that recorded the ownership of manuscripts and established the right to publish them. In accordance with this entry a second Quarto (Q2) was published in 1604, which reverted to the title of the first edition:

> The Tragical History of Hamlet, Prince of Denmark, by William Shakespeare, newly imprinted and enlarged to almost so much again as it was, according to the true and perfect copy. At London, printed by I. R. [James Roberts] for N. L. [Nicholas Ling], and are to be sold at his shop under Saint Dunstan's church in Fleet street.   1604.

Four of the seven surviving copies were printed bearing the date 1605, suggesting that printing had started late in the previous year.

Regarding the conflicting claims made by these competing publications, what follows starts with undisputed facts and what is now generally agreed. The Second Quarto, of 1604–5 (Q2), provides the fuller and more readable text and shows many signs of being printed from a manuscript in Shakespeare's own handwriting that had not been fully prepared for use in the theatre. It might well be called a 'true' version of the play as the title page says, but without being, in all senses, 'perfect'. Twentieth-century editors have called it the 'good Quarto' and the earlier publication the 'bad Quarto'.

Q1 was given its derogatory name because it is half the length of Q2 and varies in style from passages that are very close to the 'good' version to others that are awkward paraphrases, variations, or abbreviations of it, with some alternative readings of merely serviceable dialogue or ungrammatical nonsense. Its punctuation is erratic and often useless or wrong; some passages of verse are printed as prose. From some close similarities to Q2, chiefly in Act I, scholars have deduced that the manuscript was cobbled together from the report of an actor who had played Marcellus in the 'good' version. Many of these characteristics suit the description of the 'stolen and surreptitious copies, maimed and deformed by the frauds and stealths of injurious impostors' from which some early quartos had been printed, according to the editors of the First Folio collected edition of Shakespeare's plays of 1623. But this view of Q1 has recently been challenged, especially since the publication of edited reprints and Kathleen O. Irace's modernized edition in 1998. The use of the First Quarto as the acting text for a number of productions has demonstrated the theatrical viability of this earliest extant version of Shakespeare's play (see, for example, p. 150, below).

It had been argued that Roberts entered the play in the Register at the players' request to 'block' the publication of Ling's 'pirated' version and that, when that device failed, Roberts had brought out his authoritative edition, also at the players' request and using a manuscript provided by them. But we now know that the story was not that simple. The presumption that Q1 has no independent authority has been undermined by studies of other Elizabethan 'bad' quartos and by comparisons with authorial manuscripts from other times. Ernst Honigmann's *The Stability of Shakespeare's Text* (1965) showed that the very idea of one 'authentic' or 'definitive' text was anachronistic and implausible. Despite its obvious shortcomings, the First Quarto can now be seen to derive from an earlier, or an alternative, version of Shakespeare's *Hamlet*.

The Second Quarto and the later Folio are clearly superior texts but the new account of the origins of Q1 gives reason for believing that Shakespeare had at one time imagined Hamlet to be only nineteen years old, not thirty as in the other two texts. In those later versions, Yorick's skull is said to have lain in the earth three-and-twenty years but Q1 says it was for twelve years (V.i.170–8 and 11.66–83). In Q1, the clown is not asked how long he has been a grave-maker and so does not answer that it was since 'that very day that young Hamlet was born', later adding that he has been 'sexton here, man and boy, thirty years' – a time-span that fits neatly with the date given for Yorick's death (ll. 139–60). It seems plausible that Shakespeare had changed the dialogue in a second version because his idea of Hamlet had changed or to accommodate the actor Richard Burbage, who was in his thirties when he played Hamlet.

At numerous other places the First Quarto emphasizes Hamlet's youth where later texts avoid being so specific. Compare, for example, Claudius's 'All Denmark's hope, our cousin, and dearest son' with Q2's 'Our chiefest courtier, cousin, and our son' (2.32 and I.ii.117), or Ophelia's 'young prince Hamlet, the only flower of Denmark' with Q2's simpler 'Lord Hamlet' (6.40 and II.i.78), or Gertrude's 'How now, boy?' with Q2's 'Why, how now, Hamlet?' (11.8 and III.iv.14). A Hamlet considerably younger than thirty would make more credible sense of many aspects of the play. Instead of approaching fifty, his mother could be under forty years of age – still a 'frosty' age to a twenty-year-old. In performance, Ophelia frequently seems to be fifteen, half Hamlet's age, and yet the age-difference is never the subject of comment.

At twenty years of age, Rosencrantz and Guildenstern as Hamlet's 'schoolfellows' would be no older than their words and actions suggest. If Laertes, Fortinbras and Osric are also cast at about twenty years of age, with Horatio a little older, the 'young prince' and his associates will together represent a new generation rising to influence and power in the state. Even in the Q2 text, *youth* is a word that occurs more than twice as often as in *Romeo and Juliet*, which has six occurrences – a prevalence hard to explain if Hamlet was always intended to be thirty years of age. In the course of a performance with a twenty-year-old prince, the numerous occasions when young people come together without their elders provide a recurrent physical and temperamental reminder that a new Denmark is emerging, with its distinctive values and expectations.

Other differences between Q1 and later editions are not so readily explained unless Shakespeare had felt a need to make major adjustments. Claudius becomes less obviously the play's villain: in Q1, his first politically careful speech is missing and, for the final duel, he supplies all the poisons. In the 'closet scene' of the later texts (III.iv), Gertrude is less obviously ignorant of her husband's murder: she no longer assures her son, 'I never knew of this most horrid murder' (11.84). Her forthright promise of support for her son, with its echo of Kyd's *Spanish Tragedy*, is also cut:

> I will conceal, consent, and do my best,
> What stratagem soe're thou shalt devise.
>
> (11.97–8)

In Q1, however, she makes almost no contribution in the graveyard scene until after Hamlet has left the stage. Here her role is stronger in Q2 and F: it is her interjection – 'O my son, what theme?' – that receives his most lucid answer and in Q2 it is her assurance of his basic sanity – 'Anon . . . his silence will sit drooping' – that at last calms Hamlet's anger and so brings the scene to its close (see Commentary on V.i.264 and 280–4).

That Q1 is a mangled version of an earlier version of Shakespeare's play is supported by two readings. Q2's puzzling 'I the son of a dear murdered' is supplied with its missing word in Q1's equally puzzling 'I the son of my dear father' (II.ii.581). In the 'bad' Quarto, Laertes' expressed desire to tell Hamlet that 'thus he dies' (15.5) has shown editors how to emend the 'good' Quarto's almost meaningless 'The diddest thou' (IV.vii.56). It is not so remarkable, as it once had seemed, that the compositors of Q2 had recourse to Q1 (most often in Act I) when they had difficulties in reading their autograph copy. On the other hand, throughout Q1 the dialogue is so extensively mangled that all deductions about Shakespeare's early version are to some degree speculative and uncertain. When its differences from the later texts suggest alternative readings that would involve considerable changes in production, they are noted in the commentary that follows, together with a number of stage directions that seem to be eyewitness accounts of performance.

Because Q2 was printed from a manuscript in Shakespeare's own hand, most modern editions are based on its text. Some editors have

occasionally reproduced its punctuation and solved difficult cruces
by reference to quarto editions of other Shakespeare plays that were
set from similar manuscripts, and to the few samples of
Shakespeare's handwriting that have survived. In recent years,
however, some editors have based their text on the First Folio as a
text that represents Shakespeare's latest changes. Differences
between Q2 and F are given attention in the Commentary where they
could have a significant effect on performance.

The First Folio edition

Hamlet was published again in 1623, seven years after Shakespeare's
death, in the collected Folio volume of his *Comedies, Histories and
Tragedies.* Two of Shakespeare's fellow sharers in the King's Men, John
Hemmings and Henry Condell, recommended the copious volume
to readers, claiming that in place of earlier imperfect texts it offered
ones that were 'cured, and perfect of their limbs, and all the rest
absolute in their numbers as he conceived them'. The Folio text of
Hamlet (here abbreviated as F) shows signs, as does the text of Q2, that
the manuscript sent to the printers was in the author's handwriting
but of a later date, or possibly a scribal copy of such a manuscript.
The result differs frequently from the text of Q2 and has additions
and omissions that leave it shorter by some 230 lines. The compositors or a printing-house editor did not always judge their manuscript
superior to that used for Q2 since some readings in F were taken
from that earlier edition. Moreover, some of its variants seem to have
come from sources other than the author.

During the twenty years after *Hamlet* was written and first
performed any manuscript in possession of the players could have
been altered by other hands to suit the players' convenience, either
with or without an author's permission or approval, because he
would no longer be considered to 'own' the play. Consequently
editors have usually accepted the Folio's readings in preference to the
'good' Quarto's only when they judged them to be clearly superior
and possibly the author's. However, a new understanding of the
instability of theatrical texts, a preference for later editions, and a

desire to have only one authority have led some scholars to base their editions of *Hamlet* on F and accept readings from the Q2 only where F seems indefensible.

The commentary of this *Handbook* refers throughout to the New Penguin edition by T. J. B. Spencer (1980), which is based on the Second Quarto as 'the text that is closest to Shakespeare's manuscript'. Today the assumption that there was only one authorial version must be questioned but, by giving 'superior authority' to Q2, this edition does offer a text that includes all that Shakespeare wrote when the play was first performed, together with the additions of a later revision. If the commentary had followed an edition based on the Folio, extensive passages that are undoubtedly by Shakespeare would have been excluded. A full text, such as the Penguin edition, is most unlikely to have been performed in Shakespeare's own time – it would have lasted far longer than the two or three hours that were customary – but a reader of the play will surely want to have all that is available of Shakespeare's writing. Study can then be made of the different forms in which the play may originally have been performed.

An edition that follows the Folio will have shortcomings that can be justified only by a general and theoretical preference for a later manuscript over an earlier one. Many of F's variants from Q2 are barely defensible and have been rejected by most modern editors. A larger consequence would be the omission of the entry for Hamlet on his way to England in Act IV, which entails the loss of a soliloquy of 34 lines that marks a turning point in his consciousness: 'O, from this time forth, / My thoughts be bloody, or be nothing worth' (IV.iv.65–6). If Shakespeare had willingly agreed to that loss, he would also have accepted the Folio's omission of Hamlet's encounter with the Polish Captain (ll. 9–31) and consequently left a gap in the narrative and created problems in performance and stage management. The scene would have been reduced to seven and a half lines for Fortinbras, a few words in reply from his Captain, and the marching and wordless presence of his army. In the course of a play, so brief and puzzling an introduction of a person who will return to have a major role in its conclusion is without parallel in any other Shakespeare text. Q2 gives Fortinbras no more to say than does F but the Captain remains to identify him further and explain what has been happening. Fortinbras continues to have a major influence in the scene because it is his presence that gives rise to Hamlet's subsequent soliloquy in which, for the first time, he considers his own duty as a prince and the nature of greatness.

Some scholars argue that Shakespeare was responsible for all the major cuts in the Folio because, in making them, attention has been paid to metre and comprehensibility. But no great skill is needed to fit two half-lines of verse together to make one, or to make a cut at the end of a line, and still less to stop a scene before much of great consequence has happened. F's cuts frequently give rise to curious jumps in rhythm, imagery, or line of thought, for which an author whose invention was as abundant as Shakespeare's is unlikely to have been responsible: he surely would not have patched up the dialogue out of the existing text but would have re-written to the required size, as many other authors have done on other occasions (see Commentary at V.ii.105–41 and 191–212).

The seventy lines unique to the Folio are in a different category because many of them are obviously by Shakespeare. One passage may have been an accidental omission in Q2 or could have been difficult to read in the manuscript (V.ii.69–81); two others could have been deliberate omissions (see II.ii.239–69 and 336–61). Some very short phrases and unnecessary repetitions may well have been additions made by actors to extend a moment in performance or change the phrasing or timing of speech. The book-keeper could have added these to the manuscript as an aid to memory or to help actors who were being introduced to their roles after the play had settled down in the repertoire (see, for example, Commentary on III.i.92).

All matters concerning the authority of the three early texts are of interest to a reader who wishes to know how *Hamlet* might have been performed in its early days or how it can be performed at the present time, but a very full collation and lengthy notes are needed to investigate all the possibilities. The Commentary of this *Handbook* picks out those that would have a clear and significant impact on performance and considers them in the contexts in which they occur.

Early performances

The entry for a 'book of the Revenge of Hamlet' by James Roberts in the Stationers' Register on 26 July 1602 tells us that Shakespeare's play had been staged numerous times before that date. The first performance must have been more than a year earlier, sometime between the beginning of 1600 and the last months of 1599. So much can be gathered from a note written by Gabriel Harvey in a copy of Chaucer's *Works* published in 1598. This opinionated critic, pamphleteer, and fellow of Pembroke Hall, Cambridge, had bought the book in the year it was published and sometime later made a series of marginal comments, one of which records that the Earl of Essex 'commends' *Albion's England*, and adds that

> the younger sort takes much delight in Shakespeare's *Venus and Adonis*; but his *Lucrece* and his *Tragedy of Hamlet, Prince of Denmark* have it in them to please the wiser sort.

Since no one could have read the play at this time, Harvey's opinion must have been based on seeing it in performance. We do not know when each of the marginal notes was written but, since the Earl of Essex was executed for treason on 25 February 1601, this one, in the present tense, could scarcely have been made after that date. We shall see later (p. 16) that this accords with stylistic evidence that makes it all but certain that *Hamlet* was written after *Julius Caesar*, a play that can be confidently dated in 1599. Two references to Julius Caesar in *Hamlet*, one of them to a student performance (I.i.114 and III.ii.107–15), give still further support for concluding that *Hamlet* was written and first performed late in 1599 or very early in 1600.

No records of early performances exist, beyond the Stationers' Register entry and the title pages of the Quartos. Presumably it was staged at the Theatre, the predecessor of the Globe and at that time used by the Chamberlain's Men, but it would also be seen in various halls with less theatrical equipment and different audience–stage relationships. We must imagine the play's action on a platform open on three sides to an audience. It would either have been in the open or the audience lit by much the same means as the actors. Two entrances would be on either side at the rear of the acting area between which a curtain or 'arras' was hung that concealed space for at least two persons to hide (see II.ii.163). A trapdoor in the stage floor to serve as Ophelia's grave would be a near necessity but one constructed in a raised platform might possibly serve the same function, aided by some make-believe, as it often does for small-scale, present-day touring productions. A few large stage properties are required or must be improvised – two thrones and a garden bank for the Player King – and an abundance of weapons such as 'partisans', swords, and, for the final duel, rapiers.

Many costume changes are needed because they will distinguish interior from exterior scenes, formal from informal occasions, days of feasting from times of mourning, night from day. Costumes must also mark the differences between nobles, courtiers, public and private servants, students, Norwegian and Danish soldiers, seafaring men, the gravedigger and his assistant, and a priest. Ideally, Norwegian soldiers returning from war after long marches should look different from when they had arrived fresh and ready for action. Elizabethan tiring houses, used for the storing and handling of costumes, cannot have been large or well lit and so *Hamlet* would have put many strains on its staff, more than most other plays in their repertoire. Musicians were needed several times during the performance, and stage keepers to manage the properties, marshal the larger entries, and arrange for lights, cock-crow, and cannon-shot. Staging *Hamlet* would also have been a major task for the actors, who had to sustain lengthy and demanding roles or many different smaller roles that followed each other in quick succession. On tour, perhaps with fewer personnel than in their London theatre, these demands were likely to have strained the resources of the Chamberlain's and King's Men even more severely.

How the play was staged we cannot know in any detail but there is plenty of evidence that the actors performed its unusually long, inventive, and innovatory text to great acclaim. Its most demanding and problematic aspects will be considered in the commentary that follows, as well as its use of the theatre's traditional strengths of conflict, expectation, surprise, spectacle and sheer noise. That performances enjoyed a huge success is proved by five quarto editions, the frequency with which other writers of the time quoted or borrowed from it – John Marston's *Antonio's Revenge* (1601) imitates it repeatedly – and the speed with which certain phrases and word-usages entered into everyday use. We must try to envisage a varied and crowded audience responding instinctively to performance, with no press reviews or advertisements to raise expectations. It is probably safe to say that no other Elizabethan or Jacobean play was received as enthusiastically as this, and that after the death of Marlowe, very few, if any, newly written tragedies enjoyed the same popular success.

2 The Play's Sources and Cultural Context

The source of the story

We know of no single account of Hamlet that Shakespeare followed with the close attention he gave to the sources of his history plays, and of *Romeo and Juliet*, or *Julius Caesar*. What we do know is that an earlier tragedy had been performed based on the same ancient Danish saga. No text was published but the brief references that have survived are sufficient to tell us that this early *Hamlet* – the *Ur-Hamlet* as it is usually called – was very different from Shakespeare's both in story and in style. Its appeal had been crudely popular and, by following Latin models, unoriginal.

Thomas Nashe, a prolific and spirited young writer, gave the first account of an earlier *Hamlet* in a Preface to *Menaphon* (1589) by his friend Robert Greene. In a satirical attack on translators who scarcely understood Latin, which was aimed particularly at Thomas Kyd, the son of a scrivener and not a university graduate like himself, Nashe mocks those who will 'afford you whole Hamlets, I should say handfuls of tragical speeches'. He continues with a warning that 'Seneca, let blood line by line and page by page, at length must needs die to our stage.' That did not happen for a long time since, in translation, the first-century Roman dramatist continued to influence English tragedy well into the seventeenth century. And, for some years, *Ur-Hamlet* continued to hold the stage. A single performance, probably by the Chamberlain's Men, was recorded at Newington Butts on 9 June 1594. Thomas Lodge's *Wit's Misery and the World's Madness* (1596) describes the devil being 'as pale as the vizard of the ghost which cried so miserably at the Theatre, like an oyster-wife, "Hamlet, revenge!" ' The Ghost in Shakespeare's *Hamlet* does not cry out loud for all to hear, so that in this respect he did not follow the *Ur-Hamlet*. With no text surviving, its existence tells us little more than that the name Hamlet was associated with tragedies that featured passion, revenge, and lengthy speeches in a Senecan manner. Kyd's *Spanish Tragedy* and the anonymous *Arden of Faversham* were highly successful examples of this vogue, both written around 1590 and both published and several times reprinted.

As Shakespeare tells the story, its outline does have many features in common with the ancient saga as it had become known in a Latin version written by Saxo Grammaticus at the end of the twelfth century. In several passages it also comes close to a French version of the Latin by François de Belleforest in the fifth volume of his *Histoires tragiques*, published in 1570 and frequently reprinted. In this form, with its numerous additions and moralizing comments, the story was translated into English in 1608 as *The History of Hamblet*. An introductory passage, taken from the French, warns the reader that this is a pagan and brutal story:

> You must understand that, long time before the kingdom of Denmark received the faith of Jesus Christ and embraced the doctrine of the Christians, that the common people in those days were barbarous and uncivil, and their princes cruel, without faith or loyalty seeking nothing but murder and deposing or, at the least, offending each other, either in honours, goods, or lives; not caring to ransom such as they took prisoners but rather sacrificing them to the cruel vengeance naturally imprinted in their hearts.

Shakespeare's *Hamlet* is at times close to Saxo and also to Belleforest but it is unlikely that he had continuous access to either of them. We cannot know if the *Ur-Hamlet* was an intermediate source but it is clear that Shakespeare introduced major changes and additions to these published versions of the story.

In the English translation, following Belleforest, the story starts with Horvendile, the elder of two brothers and a 'most renowned pirate', who answered the challenge of Collere, the 'valiant, hardy and courageous' king of Norway, and killed him in single combat. Back in Denmark, as a reward, he was given Geruth, the Danish king's daughter, as his wife, whereupon Fengon, his younger brother, 'provoked by a foolish jealousy . . . determined (whatsoever happened) to kill him; which he effected in such sort, that no man once so much as suspected him'. Before murdering his brother, Fengon had 'incestuously abused his wife' and so it happened, after the murder, that:

> the unfortunate and wicked woman, that had received the honour to be the wife of one of the valiantest and wise[st] princes in the north, imbased herself in such vile sort as to falsify her faith unto him and, which is worse, to marry him that had been the tyrannous murderer of her lawful husband. . . . This princess, who at the first, for her rare virtues and courtesies was honoured of all men and beloved of her husband, as soon as she once gave ear to the tyrant Fengon, forgot both the rank she held among the greatest names and the duty of an honest wife. . . .

The story then passes to Hamblet, Geruth's son by her first marriage. He now feared that 'if he once attained to man's estate' Fengon would 'send him the same way as his father'. He therefore 'counterfeited the madman with such craft and subtle practises that he made show as if he had utterly lost his wits'. The pretence allowed him access to the Queen's palace where:

> he rent and tore his clothes, wallowing and lying in the dust and mire, his face all filthy and black, running through the streets like a man distraught, not speaking one word but such as seemed to proceed of madness and mere frenzy.

However, he sometimes made such fit answers that 'men of quick spirits' began to suspect that under his 'rudeness he shadowed a crafty policy'. To discover what this was, they set a 'fair and beautiful woman in a secret place . . . by all the craftiest means . . . to allure his mind to have his pleasure of her'. Hamblet was warned that this was a trap by a gentleman who had been brought up with him and also by the lady herself, who 'from her infancy loved and favoured him' and to whom Hamblet was wholly 'in affection'. Other means were used to discover Hamblet's secret, including a trick whereby he would be alone with his mother in a chamber and overheard by a 'counsellor' hiding behind the hangings. But the young prince, aware that he might betray his counterfeiting, suspected that this was another trap and:

> feeling something stirring under [the hangings], he cried, 'A rat, a rat!' and presently [*immediately*] drawing his sword thrust it into the hangings, which done, pulled the counsellor, half dead, out by the heels, made an end of killing him, and being slain, cut his body in pieces, which he caused to be boiled, and then cast it into an open vault or privy that so it might serve for food to the hogs.

The meeting between mother and son followed, as she sat 'tormenting herself' with grief and guilt. He now searched every corner of the room, 'distrusting his mother as well as the rest', and then spoke at great length in praise of his father and likening his mother to a beast in her 'unbridled desire' and second marriage. 'Be not offended, Madam,' he asked, 'if transported with dolour and grief, I speak so boldly unto you.' He then told her that he had pretended madness because he feared his uncle would kill him and that he lived to revenge his father's death. Telling her not to weep 'to see my folly, but rather sigh and lament your own offence', he then desired above all things:

> that neither the king nor any other may by any means know mine intent; and let me alone with the rest, for I hope in the end to bring my purpose to effect.

At last, 'weeping most bitterly' and gazing at her son 'as it were wholly amazed', she embraced him, confessed her guilt, warned him of the danger he was in, and promised to keep his secret and pray to the Gods for the success of his revenge.

Although the relationships between son, father, mother, and murderous uncle in Shakespeare's play have basic similarities to Belleforest's re-telling of the Danish saga, Hamlet's actions are far less brutal than Hamblet's. The latter does not simply 'lug the guts' of the counsellor he has killed into another room (*Hamlet*, III.iv.213), and, having escaped death in England and having had his companions killed in his place – a ruthless meting out of punishment that does survive in Shakespeare's play – he does not carry out his revenge in public but, after waking Fengon as he lay in his bed, by giving him 'such a blow upon the chine of the neck that he cut his head clear from his shoulder'.

Shakespeare's use of the saga

In using this sensational and violent story, Shakespeare drew upon his own highly developed sensibility and skill. His Prince Hamlet belongs to the time and culture in which he himself lived: no pagan barbarian but a gifted courtier, soldier and scholar (III.i.152), he speaks and acts so that the play could seem to be happening at the moment of performance.

When Shakespeare was writing *Hamlet*, he frequently borrowed from his own recent plays. Its meditative and impassioned soliloquies owe much to the 'still-breeding thoughts' of Richard the Second's soliloquy in prison (V.v.8) that he had written some three years earlier, and to his handling of Brutus in *Julius Caesar* of the previous year, especially the soliloquies before he joins the conspirators (II.i.10–34 and 64–9). For Hamlet's encounters with his 'fellow students', the gravedigger and, on one occasion, the king himself, Shakespeare wrote in prose – not verse as expected in tragedies – and drew upon what he had written recently for Prince Hal, Falstaff, Rosalind, Beatrice, Benedick, and many subsidiary roles. The sexual undercurrents and difficult transitions in Hamlet's talk with Ophelia and Gertrude – also highly unusual in a tragedy – look back to verbal nuances and silences charged with feeling that he had developed in a series of comedies. The performance of a play-within-the-play in *Hamlet* draws attention to the responses of its audience, as the same device does in *Love's Labour's Lost* and *A Midsummer Night's Dream*.

This tragedy's debt to earlier Shakespeare plays runs deep and wide. The addition of Laertes and Fortinbras to the story – two other sons involved with consequences of their fathers' deaths – creates an analogical and reflective dramatic structure like those of earlier histories and comedies. Recalling Henry the Fifth before Agincourt (*Henry V*, IV.i.280–502), Shakespeare's Claudius falls to his knees in the hope that the 'sweet heavens' can wash his sin as 'white as snow', whereas Fengon of the source narrative does not seem conscious of wrong-doing and seeks no remission of punishment.

In common with Senecan authors, Shakespeare did bring a ghost on stage but, as we have already seen, his spirit does not cry out furiously for revenge and it does not remain on stage to watch and comment on the action as does the Ghost of Andreas in Kyd's *Spanish Tragedy*. More like the ghost in *Julius Caesar* (IV.iii), the Ghost of Hamlet's father enters in silence and has to be challenged before speaking; in its first scene, it is said to be 'majestical' and to pass by in 'solemn march' (I.i.144 and I.ii.201). When it fades on the crowing of a cock, a soldier who has been a witness recalls the death of 'our Saviour' and by this means the play, in its opening scene, is sited unequivocally in a Christian context: no ghost in earlier tragedies had had a similar effect. In its last scene, Hamlet does not become King of Denmark, as Hamblet does; instead, as he prepares for death, he speaks of a Providence that cares for the fall of a sparrow and uses the phrasing of St Matthew's Gospel (X:29). After Hamlet's death, Horatio prays that 'flights of angels [may] sing' him to his rest. In whatever form Shakespeare encountered the story – perhaps in Belleforest or the *Ur-Hamlet* – he has made it his own and placed it in an imagined world that, in many ways, was like that of his audience.

Shakespeare also illuminated its action by borrowing from many literary sources available at the time so that his Hamlet became what today would be called an intellectual, a young man alert to the political and personal issues of the day. Before he hears of his father's Ghost he is intent on going 'back to school in Wittenberg' (I.ii.112–13), a university famed in Shakespeare's day for the teaching of the church reformer Martin Luther, and at which Marlowe imagined Faustus earning his doctorate. Those among Shakespeare's fellow playwrights who became known as the 'university wits' had come to London to live by their writing in their early or mid-twenties. Young men of privileged background who went to Oxford or Cambridge, usually left much earlier. Henry Wriothesley, Earl of Southampton and Shakespeare's patron, had left St John's College, Cambridge, with his M.A. a few months before his sixteenth birthday and then proceeded to Gray's Inn, London, to study law. Earlier, in 1581, Robert

Devereux, the Earl of Essex, had graduated from Trinity College, Cambridge, just after his sixteenth birthday. The play is full of the learning sought and used among Shakespeare's well-educated contemporaries and, for a prince, Hamlet is unusually given to study and intellectual discourse. His speeches and soliloquies have the accents and processes of active thought – the 'quick forge and working-house of thought' (*Henry V*, Act V, Prol., l. 23) – and his choice of words seems to be uniquely his own.

Some of the play's occasional sources have been traced (see, especially, Muir, *Sources*, pp. 166–70). In creating the Ghost, Shakespeare would have been mindful of tragedies by Seneca and Thomas Kyd but he also turned to the translation *Of Ghosts and Spirit* by Ludwig Lavater, which had reached a second edition in 1596. For Osrick, the 'waterfly' courtier (V.ii.83), and for allusions to Danish drunkenness, he seems to have borrowed from Thomas Nashe's *Pierce Penniless, his Supplication to the Devil* (1592). For Hamlet's melancholy, he drew upon Timothy Bright's *Treatise of Melancoly* (1586). Here, for instance, melancholics are said to be attracted to suicide as a means to 'avoid the terror' of desperation and are recommended to use the 'custom of exercises' (II.ii.296–7). We may understand Hamlet's behaviour better if we recognize the symptoms of melancholy identified by Bright, which include false laughter, fearful and terrible dreams, fantastical apparitions, and long deliberations: 'the whole force of the spirit [is] closed up in the dungeon of melancholy darkness' (for similar ideas in *Hamlet*, see II.ii.243 and 253–5). Such echoes could be accidental but Hamlet's remark that 'I am but mad north-north-west. When the wind is southerly, I know a hawk from a handsaw' (II.ii.377–8) does seem to depend on Bright's *Treatise*:

> the air meet for melancholic folk ought to be thin, pure and subtle, open and patent to all winds: in respect of their temper, especially to the South and South-east.

Still more echoes can be heard in the text from the *Essays* of Michel de Montaigne. Although Florio's translation would have been available only in manuscript, Shakespeare might have had access to that in the household of his and Florio's patron, the Earl of

Southampton. (The book was published in 1603 after being entered in the Stationers' Register on 4 June 1600.) The titles of some of the essays might be used to delineate Hamlet's intellectual concerns: 'our affections are transported beyond our selves ... the taste of Goods and Evils doth greatly depend on the opinion we have of them ... the vanity of words ... bad means employed to a good end'. Montaigne's scepticism, his concern with the nature of truth, honesty and fame, his conscience and questioning of both himself and others, and his repeated contemplation of death have many parallels with Hamlet's soliloquies and intellectual restlessness. It cannot be proved that Shakespeare had read Montaigne at this time – as he certainly had by the time he wrote *King Lear* and *The Tempest* – but it can confidently be said that the two authors had many of the same concerns, including the nature of truth and the difficulty of seeking it. In *Hamlet* can be heard echoes of many books of philosophy, practical knowledge, and controversy that were in print at the time and might have been sought out by a leisured scholar like Montaigne or by a writer of wide intellectual interests and ambition, like Shakespeare.

Prince Hamlet shares the mentality and, to a large extent, the language of the most gifted and adventurous writers of Shakespeare's England: Spenser, Sidney, Donne and Raleigh among the poets, Marlowe, Jonson, Chapman and Webster among dramatists. In their works and in Hamlet's discourse can be found the same range of closely related ideas about matters of life and death, knowledge and uncertainty, fate and free will, society and individuals, justice and mercy, time and space, the sky, earth, and ocean. In this Hamlet is exceptional because no other person in Shakespeare's plays has been given such range and immediacy of thought: the hero of a pagan saga has become a person with a conscience that is like those of the finest spirits of the age.

Personal, social, and political contexts

This play reflected the life that Shakespeare lived as well as the books he had read and, although tracing its influence is even more difficult, the effect of his life-experience was the greater in shaping dramatic structure and giving life to the persons on stage.

(i)   'A Cry of Players'

The one aspect of Shakespeare's day-to-day experience that has left obvious marks on the text of the play is the time he spent in theatres as actor and part-owner of both theatre and company, as well as being its principal author. The dialogue of *Hamlet* includes much theatre terminology and word-usage; and its action frequently requires an audience as well as performers.

Kyd's *Spanish Tragedy*, already mentioned as a possible source, concludes with a play organized by its revenging hero and re-presenting the principal events of the story, but *The Murder of Gonzalo*, staged at the request of Hamlet, comes long before the final scene and its professional actors contribute more than that performance. They are seen as they arrive at court and are welcomed by Hamlet; before they are led to their lodgings, the 'First Player' gives a 'taste' of his talent in an old play. They are seen again, and again with Hamlet present, as they prepare for performance. The play itself is inter-rupted, ending in disorder and forsaken by its audience. This leaves Hamlet highly excited, declaiming in rhymed verse, and thinking of himself as one in 'a cry of players' (III.ii.28off.). In an unprecedented way, the tragedy uses its author's first-hand experience to reveal the consequences of playing with the 'false fire' of performance (III.ii.275).

Many scenes in *Hamlet* draw upon Shakespeare's intimate knowledge and experience of the theatre, often in unusual ways. The Ghost in the first scene is no actor but, because it says nothing, those who watch are left trying to grasp what the dumb show has meant. In doing so they reveal their own concerns and instinctive reactions:

> 'Tis gone and will not answer.

> How now, Horatio? You tremble and look pale.

And again:

It was about to speak when the cock crew.
And then it started, like a guilty thing
Upon a fearful summons. . . .

                                        (I.i.52–3 and 148–50)

In the second scene, Claudius and Gertrude are performers, their private thoughts disguised rather than expressed; the theatre audience is given only hints of this so that individual spectators are left to make what sense they can of what is shown on stage. But meanwhile Hamlet very clearly identifies his pretence. No 'forms, moods, shapes of grief' can denote him truly:

            These indeed 'seem';
For they are actions that a man might play.
But I have that within which passes show –
These but the trappings and the suits of woe.

                                        (I.ii..76–86)

This theatrical metaphor is carried forward in a repeated use of *show* and *seem* and in talk of the 'change [of] name' and standing dumb with 'the act of fear' (see ll. 163 and 204–6).

In moments of both calculation and passion, even with no Players at hand to prompt him, Hamlet is conscious of himself as an actor. He says he will 'put an antic disposition on' and, before performing this way in public, demonstrates how he will do this and what response he is likely to get (I.v.170–9). When his friends seem not to understand his question, he is aware of their bad performance, a 'kind of confession in [their] looks' showing him that they do not have 'craft enough to colour' their thoughts (II.ii.269–80). As the tragedy draws towards its close, theatrical metaphors continue to inform what Hamlet says: 'an thou'lt mouth, / I'll rant as well as thou' (V.i.279–80); before 'I could make a prologue to my brains / They had begun the play' (V.ii.30–1). In the last scene, he appears before the whole court, as the players had done, and fights in a duel which has been secretly rigged: as he lies mortally wounded, he sees the onlookers as 'mutes or audience to this act', both silent performers in the event and innocent spectators (V.ii.328–9). In the tragedy's last minutes Horatio orders that the dead bodies 'High on a stage be

placèd to the view' and promises to tell the 'yet unknowing world /
How these things came about' (V.ii.371–4).

(ii)   *The Court*

When the Chamberlain's men performed at the Court of Elizabeth I,
in one of the royal palaces, Shakespeare gained experience of life in
the privileged, protected, and busy enclave that was the source of
political power in England. Today it is difficult to imagine that little
world where just one person exercised an absolute authority
throughout the larger world outside, but this was the context in
which Shakespeare imagined the action of *Hamlet*. At the start of Act
III, scene iii, he allowed Rosencrantz and Guildenstern sufficient time
to remind the theatre audience that the play took place at the power
centre of the country: they are trying to impress the King, who has no
need to hear what he already knows:

> GUILDENSTERN   Most holy and religious fear it is
>   To keep those many many bodies safe
>   That live and feed upon your majesty.
> ROSENCRANTZ   The single and peculiar life is bound
>   With all the strength and armour of the mind
>   To keep itself from noyance; but much more
>   That spirit upon whose weal depends and rests
>   The lives of many. The cess of majesty   [*cease of royal authority*]
>   Dies not alone, but like a gulf doth draw
>   What's near it with it . . .
>   Never alone
>   Did the king sigh, but with a general groan.
>
>   (III.i.8–23)

Hamlet's fellow students are saying that everyone is threatened by
Hamlet's seeming madness because the King is threatened by it.

Shakespeare's observation of life at Court has left many other
marks throughout the play. As with the theatrical, this courtly
context is established early when the whole cast assembles at the
start of the second scene for a formal royal occasion that is in strong
contrast with the talk of sentries on night duty in the 'bitter cold'

(I.i.8) and their frightened reactions to the silent ghost. Claudius, in full regalia, controls the entire proceedings, speaking at length with careful assurance. The '*Council*' (Q2, S.D.) and attendants are, for the most part, silent and respectful observers; they are in 'the presence' and, were the King to 'sigh', they would respond with 'a general groan'. The gathering is for policy announcements and giving thanks; after dealing with a number of matters, the King leaves to drink and celebrate. In Elizabeth or Jacobean performances, members of the Court would animate the action by marking the more significant passages of his speech with individually improvised responses. When two ambassadors receive a limited 'scope' of the King's 'personal power' (I.ii.33–8), they would probably approach, kiss his hand and then retire ten feet to hear their commission, bowing low before taking their leave. Demonstrative ceremonies of this kind were common at Court, as described in letters of the time (see, for example, Bullough, pp. 185–7). In these ways, a real-life context for the tragedy would be established.

Elizabeth's Court also saw many private meetings between the monarch and her chief councillors. *Hamlet* includes a number of these, both pre-arranged and having varying degrees of formality, and unscheduled, when everything is improvised: in all of them the King will be the central figure and arbitrator. Often the persons in attendance will be apprehensive: for example, Polonius tells Ophelia to go with him to the King (II.i.117) but, in the event, he brings with him only one of Hamlet's letters as evidence of his daughter's predicament. The re-emergence of Claudius and Polonius after they had withdrawn to watch Ophelia 'encounter' Hamlet, allows no opportunity for her to speak her mind. Having noticed her presence, her father only tells her that she need not say anything: in this context, she is, in effect, a non-person. The one-to-one meetings between Laertes and Claudius (IV.v.201–19 and IV.vii.1–161) break court protocol for both subject and 'majesty': in unforeseen circumstances, after political insurrection and personal distress, both find themselves having to improvise physically and mentally out of their usual roles. They speak at length but with care and trepidation: the King talks of his marriage as if uncertain of his part in it; Laertes is assured in his response, speaking with a brevity that is almost disrespectful and, therefore, dangerous.

In their first scene, Claudius assures Hamlet that he is 'Our chiefest courtier, cousin, and our son' (I.ii.117) and yet those who know the ways of the Court will see very clearly that this is not so. Hamlet is repeatedly alone, visited in private and spied on by his friends: speaking 'like an honest man', he says he is 'most dreadfully attended' by his servants (II.ii.268–9). Shakespeare has used solitariness as an expression of Hamlet's mind and also to indicate the unusual and dangerous situation in which he finds himself. Repeatedly time is taken to set the scene socially and politically. For example, after seeing his father's ghost, he is immediately aware that he is alone among people who will be concerned with other business:

> And so, without more circumstance at all,
> I hold it fit that we shake hands and part:
> You, as your business and desire shall point you,
> For every man hath business and desire,
> Such as it is; and for my own poor part
> I will go pray.

(I.v.127–32)

Normally, at Court, persons stay together to observe and be observed. John Donne's *Satire* IV, written in the late 1590s, describes the courtier as a person who is never alone and so knows:

> When the Queen frown'd, or smil'd, and he knows what
> A subtle statesman may gather of that;
> He knows who loves whom; and who by poison
> Hastes to an office's reversion; . . .
> He like a privileg'd spy, whom nothing can
> Discredit, libels now 'gainst each great man.
> He names a price for every office paid; . . .
> Who wastes in meat, in clothes, in horse, he notes;
> Who loves whores, who boys, and who goats.

(ll. 99–128)

Satire will exaggerate but has an underlying truth. Elsinore, like any royal Court of the time, is surely a place for spying, wasteful indulgence, constant competition for notice and favour, and a necessary secrecy. Polonius, giving serious and lengthy instructions to

Laertes and, subsequently, to Reynaldo (I.iii.58–80 and II.i.1–73), spells out these expectations. Laertes, too, sets out the nature of court life when he warns his sister that a prince can 'Carve for himself', unlike 'unvalued persons' (I.iii.11–44). Horatio has 'no revenue' and, therefore, no need to flatter like a courtier; Hamlet values his friendship because court life means nothing to him. He can:

> . . . let the candied [*sweet-talking*] tongue lick absurd pomp,
> And crook the pregnant hinges of the knee
> Where thrift [*profit*] may follow fawning.
>
> (III.ii.66–72)

In soliloquy, Hamlet catalogues, among more personal afflictions, some of the same corruptions of the Court in terms more sober and indignant that Donne's:

> Th'oppressor's wrong, the proud man's contumely, . . .
> The insolence of office, and the spurns
> That patient merit of th'unworthy takes.
>
> (III.i.71–4)

Watching the gravedigger, Hamlet imagines that a skull is that of:

> a courtier, which could say 'Good morrow, sweet lord! How dost thou, sweet lord?' This might be my Lord Such-a-one, that praised my Lord Such-a-one's horse when 'a meant to beg it, might it not?
>
> (V.i.81–5)

To understand *Hamlet* in its context, we have to understand what its text does not say in so many words: that Hamlet is alert at all times to deceit and aware of the King's undisputed power. He is, very precisely, 'be-netted round with villainies' (V.ii.29) – meaning that he is inescapably involved with the hidden and dangerous subtleties of the Court. The prime example is demonstrated in action not words, since Osrick almost always uses words as if they were a frivolous ornamentation. He is the typical courtier, having 'much land, and fertile', a beast whose 'crib shall stand at the king's mess'. In Hamlet's view, he is 'a chough', or rich fool, who is only 'spacious in the possession of dirt' (V.ii.86–9). But that is to underestimate him. Osrick is an emissary of the King and the play's action shows him to be responsible for taking charge of the duel in such a way that Leartes can take the unbated rapier. He also knows before everyone else that Fortinbras is about to enter in the last moments of the play, and that he comes with conquest from Poland and greets the English Ambassadors with a 'warlike volley' (V.ii.344–6). As John Webster was to say of the Court in King James's time:

> In such slippery ice-pavements, men had need
> To be frost-nailed well; they may break their necks else.
>
> *(The Duchess of Malfi, V.ii.333–4)*

(iii)   *London*

Clearly and repeatedly *Hamlet* is located in Elsinore where the King of Denmark holds his Court and yet in a few scenes everything could be happening in Shakespeare's London, and the playwright's experience of that city is another influence on the writing of the play. At first an audience may not know where the action takes place; were it not for non-English names, the change of a guard could be in London or anywhere else, in the winter of any year. Then, with talk of a ghost, another location is established that might well be a 'fantasy' (I.i.23) before becoming unequivocally Denmark. The arrival of the Players in Act II provides the first of two sustained occasions when the play can seem to be taking place in London rather than Denmark. For a few minutes, the audience in the theatre find themselves watching persons on stage watching a performance, and seeming to live in a space similar to their own, in London and at the present time.

A yet more complete shift to London occurs at the beginning of the last Act. Not only is a graveyard a recognizable part of any large community but one of the two clowns who enter would have had a face and presence known to almost all theatregoers in Shakespeare's London. He was probably Robert Armin, the creator of Touchstone in *As You Like It* and Feste in *Twelfth Night*, famous for his odd physical appearance and the ability to engage directly with his audience. And yet, however familiar he may be, the First Clown, or gravedigger, will also be a surprise to the audience, because no person in the play so far, except perhaps the nameless 'Seafaring men' (IV.vi.2), has spoken in such a familiar way. With his arrival the dialogue starts to refer to very ordinary lives and their hopes and fears, to salvation, legal judgments, the privileges of 'great folk', and the finality of death.

As soon as the grave-maker arrives on stage Shakespeare uses the social context of performance to bring Hamlet's situation home to a London audience. The laboured humour of the clown's riddle – 'What is he that builds stronger than either the mason, the shipwright, or the carpenter?' (V.i.41–2) – springs to life with the Second Clown's unexpected answer, 'The gallows-maker.' Today this alternative is more strained than the correct answer – the grave-maker – but, besides 'do[ing] well to those that do ill' (ll. 46–9), the reference to a gallows would take the minds of the play's first audiences out of the theatre and into the streets of London. The makers of both graves and gallows were more familiar sights than royalty or courtiers. Life expectancy was short and minor crimes were punishable with death. On the recurrent Law days it was said that 'at least twenty or thirty men and women' were hanged in the city of London for theft, larceny, and other offences. Gallows were erected at either end of Fetter Lane in the heart of the city. At the southern end of London Bridge the heads of traitors were displayed on staves and would stay there until they were rotten, when they were thrown into the Thames. In 1602, when *Hamlet* was playing, a traveller from overseas counted thirty mouldering heads; in 1592 there had been thirty-four (see Gordon Home, *Old London Bridge* (1931), pp. 154–5).

Hamlet was written at a time of lawlessness when many determined attempts were being made to curb vagrant and 'masterless' men in an effort to make the capital a safer place, as it grew ever richer through the work of merchants and speculators in property. Many would say that 'The time is out of joint' and wonder who, or what, might 'set it right' (I.v.188–9).

(iv)　The countryside and Stratford-upon-Avon

While not represented on stage, the context in which the play was written included the English countryside where Shakespeare had grown up and would spend most of his last years. Present-day Stratford-upon-Avon retains only a few physical remnants from the 1560s and 1570s when he was a child, and nothing of the way of life then. At that time, the town's six or seven streets housed about two hundred families and probably fewer than a thousand adults. Its group of buildings was surrounded by open fields, and Saxton's map of Warwickshire (1576) shows that much of the northern half of the county was well wooded. Shakespeare's father and mother had come from the country to live by trade and they prospered in the town, which was then growing in size and wealth, but, from their house, the countryside remained within close view and was easily accessible. During his last years Shakespeare retired from London to Stratford, living in a large house of ten rooms that he had bought in 1597. The sights and sounds of life in rural England lay deep in his memory and, from time to time, emerged in the dialogue he wrote, even when the play's action was at Court or in London.

At the end of *Hamlet*'s first scene on the battlements of Elsinore, Horatio directs attention to the sky and distant hills:

> But look, the morn in russet mantle clad
> Walks o'er the dew of yon high eastward hill.
>
> (I.i.167–8)

'Russet' and 'dew' speak to the senses of sight and touch; 'clad' and 'walks' give a familiar physicality to an imagined landscape at the start of a winter's morning. In the third scene, still at Elsinore, the country-side takes over from thoughts of politics, warfare, and court society:

> The canker galls the infants of the spring
> Too oft before their buttons [*buds*] be disclosed;
> And in the morn and liquid dew of youth
> Contagious blastments are most imminent.
>
> (I.iii.39–42)

The language is decorous and stiff and yet the images and memories it awakens are physical, sensuous, and sustained. In the fifth scene as the Ghost is about to leave, another brief reference to the dawn carries a minutely observed and sensory memory:

The glow-worm shows the matin to be near
And 'gins to pale his uneffectual fire.

(I.v.89–90)

Life outside a large city has a rare but repeated presence in the dialogue through much of the play (see, for example, II.ii.298–303 and III.iv.60, 65–8, and 152) and then, in the last two Acts, it makes a far stronger impression with Ophelia's madness, her off-stage death, and her funeral. 'Grass-green turf . . . mountain snow . . . sweet flowers' establish the countryside setting of her thoughts (IV.v.31–8); the herbs and flowers she has gathered and distributes imply that she has gone out of doors into a garden. The first line of a popular song that she sings, 'For bonny sweet Robin is all my joy' (IV.v.187), probably refers to Robin Hood, the folk hero of the greenwood (see, for example, *As You Like It*, I.i.105–9). Gertrude reports Ophelia's death while garlanded with wild flowers and chanting 'snatches of old tunes' as if it were in a world of 'liberal shepherds' and 'cold maids', the river pulling her to a 'muddy death' (IV.vii.166–83). While Gertrude speaks, the action on stage is stilled, as if everyone is aware of their distance from Ophelia. In the following scene, Gertrude brings flowers to the funeral and lets them fall onto the body in the open grave.

(v)   Religion

The tragedy that had its origins in a pagan story about the pursuit of revenge is influenced from start to finish by the ideas and practices of Christianity that forbid the taking of revenge. Religion was hugely important in Shakespeare's day, leading men and women to face death with courage, causing wars and persecution, influencing and sometimes directing the most important political decisions, and marking the course of everyone's lives with its annual sequence of observances. In England, weekly attendance at church was required by law and the celebrations of birth, marriage, and death were formulated by the officially approved Book of Common Prayer. Almost everyone believed in the existence of a supernatural world and life after death. Many would take it for granted that a divine providence guided or controlled their individual lives. These fundamental matters of thought and behaviour will rarely be found unaltered or unquestioned anywhere in the world today whereas, in Shakespeare's time, they were ubiquitous. Although variously interpreted and increasingly questioned, religious belief and practice were matters of life and death for almost everyone. Their presence can be sensed time and again in *Hamlet*, as in almost all plays of the time, and how much weight or certainty attaches to each occasion should exercise the minds of every reader or performer who wishes to understand significant implications of its text.

Inevitably, religion figured largely in the cultural context of a play about revenge and especially in Hamlet's deliberations about death, consciousness, and personal responsibility. But theology is never the prime subject of *Hamlet*, as it is in Spanish plays of the same period, neither does the play's outcome offer its hero a choice between Heaven and Hell, as in Marlowe's *Dr Faustus*. Religion is so interfused with other issues in Shakespeare's play and its values are so often ambiguously or uncertainly presented that these matters need to be considered with close reference to the text. They will be a continuing concern in the commentary that follows (see especially, significant passages at I.i.141–2 and 143–66; I.v.1–9; III.iii.36–72; III.iv.141–57; and V.ii.203–17).

3 *Commentary*

ACT I

Act I, scene i

Battlements, a bitterly cold night, a clock striking twelve, challenges and recognitions, with worried and sceptical consultation about a ghost, all silenced by the entry of a commanding figure in complete armour: these details from the first scene of *Hamlet* have become clichés for dramatists, storytellers, poets, and film-makers. But when first brought together the effect on an audience might well have been to 'harrow' it with fear and wonder (l. 44), as it does Horatio, Hamlet's fellow scholar from university.

Even today, when performed with clarity in each moment, this opening can cast a spell and start the play's action in a context that extends far beyond the bounds of ordinary time and space, to ancient Rome, the past history of Denmark and Norway, the royal palace, active military workshops, and the betrayal of Christ that led to his death. At the end of the scene, as those who have seen the Ghost of his father go off to seek 'young Hamlet' (l. 171), the focus of attention narrows and preparation for the tragic hero's entrance is almost complete.

1–13 The relieving soldier makes the challenge, not the one on guard who should do so. Incomplete verse-lines indicate pauses, after 'heart' and before or after 'good night', that can give a sense of unease or, perhaps, foreboding. So, too, can Bernardo's concern that two comrades 'make haste' to join him.

14–22 The approach of Horatio and Marcellus immediately on cue, the challenge, and the recognitions that follow quicken the pace and

31

relieve the earlier, half-spoken tension. Horatio's odd response (l. 19) followed by Marcellus's question about 'this thing' can sound ominous but will probably be more credible if spoken lightly, consciously holding back deeper concerns. Barnardo's 'I have seen nothing' (l. 22) can hardly be reassuring because he has only just taken over the watch; the incomplete verse-line indicates a shared silence before Marcellus has the first sustained speech in the play.

23–34 Horatio, a scholar among soldiers, maintains the contrasting and sceptical presence suggested by his first few words: 'Tush, tush' is casually, perhaps scornfully, dismissive (l. 29). Marcellus, with 'fantasy . . . dreaded . . . apparition' begins to clarify his earlier 'thing' (l. 21).

In early performances they might 'sit down' on the empty stage, forming a small group that drew a close dramatic focus.

35–52 After a pause, Barnardo draws attention to the night sky, high above their heads, and so deflects attention from the Ghost's entry.

At line 42 the others turn towards Horatio who is a changed man, struck now by 'fear and wonder'. Everyone will have risen to his feet. When the Ghost makes some sign (see l. 45), Horatio, encouraged by the others, asks a direct and respectful question. When it is silent and 'stalks away', he tries to take 'charge' by demanding an answer.

53–69 Horatio is left trembling and speechless until, after a half-line pause, he answers Barnardo as if on oath before his 'God'. Pressed by Marcellus to confirm what they all have seen, he takes time before replying and then a silence follows (l. 64). Having voiced concern for what the 'strange' phenomenon (l. 64) bodes for Denmark, he is again silent. All three are left standing (see l. 70), amazed and frightened.

70–111 Again they sit and again Marcellus supplies crucial information, this time about the warlike state of Denmark, a topic that Horatio takes up at greater length, speaking carefully with numerous subordinate clauses, parentheses, qualifications, and some displacement of normal word order. By this means Shakespeare has ensured that the audience pays close attention to the exposition or, at least, knows that the play will be concerned with an involved and long-standing political situation and, notably, with fathers and sons.

112–25   Horatio's scepticism returns but in the minds of his audience, both on stage and in the theatre, his account of cataclysmic portents in ancient Rome will set a cosmic scene for the Ghost's reappearance.

This speech and Barnardo's preceding one are not in F, for which the narrative does not suffer; some editors argue that actors made the cut to shorten performance or because the digression had not held the audience's attention.

126–40   Reaction to the Ghost's second appearance is very different from that to the first. Horatio at once, and on his own initiative, confronts its approach, even though standing in the way of a ghost or spirit was thought to incur malevolent consequences. Presumably it does halt on 'Stay, illusion' because that command is not repeated. At first Horatio does not assume that it has any real presence but, in their sequence, his four calls for it to speak suggest a growing belief in its reality and real-life past. By the time he orders an armed soldier to 'Stop it' (l. 140), he must have assumed that it has some kind of physical reality.

The stage direction following line 127 in the Penguin and other editions is an emendation of '*It spreads his arms*' in Q2, where it is placed opposite lines 127 to 129. Since *his* was used normally for the modern *its*, Q2's direction probably indicates that Horatio has dared to approach the Ghost.

The '*cock crows*' as if on cue to prevent Horatio mentioning the call for revenge, which was considered a prime reason why a ghost might appear (as in the *Ur-Hamlet*; see pp. 12–13, above).

141–2   For a moment Marcellus turns to Horatio, during which time the Ghost moves away so that Barnardo has to re-direct their attention. Consternation and hurried movement among the three persons on stage can take the audience's attention away from the Ghost at the moment of its disappearance so that the effect may seem magical or supernatural. But technical stage devices are often used with the same purpose: a trapdoor and smoke would have been available in early performances; today, with a projected image standing in for the Ghost, it can, very literally, fade into nothing.

143–66   Horatio finds 'probation' [*proof*] for a common superstition: see the example of Flibbertigibbet, who is said to walk 'till the first cock' (*King Lear*, III.iv.104–5). But Shakespeare may have invented the belief that it sang all night at Christmas, since scholars have found no other reference to this superstition: its effect is to widen the historical and ideological context of the play's opening scene. The sceptical Horatio's partial belief (see l. 166) lends the notion some authority here, as does Marcellus's sustained and careful speech.

167 to the end   The awed aftermath of the Ghost's appearance, with its longer speech rhythms, and the switch of attention to an imagined off-stage dawn, both serve to accentuate the brisk speech and decisive action that follow. Expectation is drawn forward to the report that will be given to 'young Hamlet', the play's eponymous hero.

Act I, scene ii

The first Act climaxes slowly towards the Ghost's message and his son's impassioned response but, before that and within those overarching concerns, more particular personal and political issues are presented as this scene moves from a crowded public occasion to Hamlet's first soliloquy and then to his meeting with the three who had left the stage at the end of scene i. Least expected will be the exposure of Hamlet's very inward and private predicament, which even he cannot fully understand.

1–16   Trumpets immediately register a striking change of place, time, and mood but a considerable length of time will be necessary for everyone to come on stage in appropriate order and take up their proper places for a public meeting with the Danish king. Almost all the available actors will be involved and two thrones, with perhaps a dais, will be carried on. Since this is a celebratory occasion, every one will be in their finest clothes, except Hamlet, who is dressed in black. The King and Queen will wear their crowns and, probably, special ceremonial robes. However, some unease may be felt among early theatre audiences because this king has 'taken' his late brother's wife as his own wife, a re-marriage that in Shakespeare's day had to receive special dispensation from the church.

Claudius's speech is masterly; a long sentence that has no need of a full stop until line 116. He uses a variety of metaphors and moves easily between past and present times, public and private matters, 'delight and dole'. Gertrude's silence, as she sits on a throne beside him, is in strong contrast. How she reacts will be closely watched when her new husband draws attention to her at line 8 and is entirely at the actor's discretion. Claudius may dwell for a moment on her presence (he often takes her hand, sometimes kissing it) but then turns away to continue his address to the assembly. The moment of contact, however brief, is like a spotlight on their relationship.

During the speech, the persons on stage are free to react, individually or together, thereby establishing the Court's relationship to 'majesty' and its autocratic power.

17–41 As Claudius speaks of what his council already knows (lines 17 to 26), attention on stage may slacken, but for the theatre audience the details are new and some spectators will want to follow closely. The Ambassadors will step forward when they are named, to kneel and receive their commission, which gives them the power to negotiate for the King. The pause indicated by the incomplete verse-line probably marks their rising and stepping back to their places (see p. 23, above).

42–63 When Laertes is called, it is his turn to approach and kneel before Claudius or, in present-day productions, to show his loyalty to the King in some other way. Perhaps Polonius also steps forward to stand beside his son or, on this occasion, just behind him. 'My *dread* lord' is unusual in this play and may indicate that Laertes is overplaying his subservience in an effort to get what he wants. (Q1 has the more usual 'gracious'.) Perhaps his father's permission had indeed been given after a great deal of persuasion but, on the other hand, Polonius may be putting the most loyal possible appearance on his son's desire to go off to Paris (see ll. 58–9).

Claudius's wish and admonishment (ll. 62–3) have a flagging rhythm so that, in performance, he may seem to envy the young man his freedom, having already felt the constraints that come with power. Alternatively, he may be thinking of the problems posed by Hamlet, the fatherless son, before he turns to address him.

64–7 '*Aside*' is a modern editor's addition to the original texts. The actor should feel free to choose whether Hamlet's first and conspicuously short speech gives him a private, bitterly humorous satisfaction or whether it is an open and outspoken challenge to the smooth words of his new stepfather, spoken either impulsively or in a calculated manner. However this speech is delivered, the dramatic focus is suddenly and for the first time centred on the stubbornly black-clad son of the 'dear brother' to whom Claudius has referred briefly, and whose ghost the audience has already seen.

Hamlet's few words are strongly against the tide of events as Claudius is marshalling them, and contrary to his manner of speaking. The two confront each other, no matter how far they are apart or how smoothly Hamlet has addressed the King. The pun on *son/sun* ensures that the stand-off finishes strongly, with the emphasis on Hamlet's double meanings and private feelings.

68–75 Gertrude's speech is delicately balanced and can be spoken in many ways. It could be crafty since 'Denmark' avoids overt reference to her own relationship to the new king and to her ex-husband; yet the phrasing and rhythm of speech are untroubled and, while speaking of death, she also speaks of a new life in heaven as if having the solace and faith of a devout Christian. In performance, she can seem insensitive to her son's feelings, glossing over all difficulties, or deeply and intuitively in sympathy with him, using gentle words to soften the brute facts; she may seem to hover between these alternatives.

Hamlet's first response is so phrased that its complaisant words can bristle with a suppressed anger, resentment, incredulity, or pain.

For a second time, two of the principals in the tragedy confront each other, as Gertrude's rejoinder confirms.

76–86   The short phrases, repetitions, and two negatives of Hamlet's first sustained speech ensure that it seems to burst out, highly charged and instinctive, however controlled it is in performance. While he then takes his time, as if avoiding close confrontation, his words are barbed: 'good mother' echoes his mother's 'Good Hamlet', and 'customary . . . forced . . . fruitful . . . dejected' all carry implicit criticisms of her 'behaviour'. Responding to these words in the context of the whole play, the actor may show that Hamlet takes pleasure or comfort in the idea of 'play' and an actor's skill in hiding his own feelings.

As the linked elements of the speech unfold without hesitation and conclude comprehensively, everyone on stage and in the theatre will be drawn to listen and watch. Much depends on how close mother and son are to each other physically when she becomes silent or finds herself wanting to reply but unable to do so.

87–117   By re-asserting his control over the situation, whether with political cunning or in harsh self-interest, Claudius steps into the very centre of the personal confrontation between his new bride and her son, taking over with words of flattery and smooth urbanity. He then proceeds once again to demonstrate his mastery of words and argument, only this time 'obstinate . . . impious stubbornness . . . unmanly' are outspoken reproofs. Hamlet making no response, he then develops his criticism of him with reasoned argument that appeals to theology and to 'vulgar' or common sense. He sharpens what is now an attack, with 'peevish' and the dismissive 'Fie,' before turning to the more considerate 'We pray you . . .' and presenting himself as a new 'father' (ll. 106–8). At this point the speech becomes ostensibly public and political – 'For, let the world take note . . .' – while reaching its most personal appeal as from a 'dearest father' to his son (ll. 110–11).

118–20   When Claudius spoke of Hamlet's 'intent' to return to Wittenberg University (ll. 112–13), using the most persuasive terms he knows, Hamlet had made no reply, but now Gertrude intervenes with a personal appeal simply expressed. With all eyes on him, Hamlet's one-line submission is verbally simple too, but with a qualification that reserves his independence. Again, dramatic focus is brought to bear piercingly on the physical and emotional relationship of these two principal persons in the tragedy: this time Claudius intervenes.

121–8   Now Claudius speaks complacently and in good spirits, but each element is briefly, almost brusquely, expressed despite representing an about-turn. In the context of performance, 'This gentle and unforced accord of Hamlet' (l. 123) is so against the facts that it will sound hollowly as an example of the 'plastering art' of words (see III.i.51). Claudius's final 'Come away' sets everyone moving, any disharmony covered (according to Q2) by a '*Flourish*' of trumpets.

129–59   As the crowd disperses, Hamlet is left alone, perhaps unmoving. His body is the first thing he speaks about, not his mother or recently dead father, or the new king. Possibly it is his sexual yearning that, consciously or unconsciously, he means by 'flesh'. Or he might use the word in a New Testament and Pauline sense, meaning his propensity to sin. The metaphors that follow are all taken from physical or bodily phenomena but his next thought is of suicide so that hopelessness and self-reproach are, surely, Hamlet's residual reactions. The actor's performance is likely to respond freely to these feelings, expressing the unease by physical as well as verbal means.

Calling twice on 'God' (l. 132) may be a casual expression of hopelessness but the name of God was not invoked lightly in the public theatres: here it leads on to the image of an untended garden, which implies forgetfulness, shame, or self-loathing. Alternatively, 'God' could be a form of protest, carrying on the previous line's opposition to the will of 'the Everlasting'.

Besides striking figures of speech, often implying a very physical imagination and response, this soliloquy has a seemingly natural movement of thought and feeling, with repetitions, corrections, exclamations, and quick changes of intention. Some apparently artless and instinctive expressions imply tender and personal feelings; others again imply revulsion, hatred, and a sense of despair or helplessness. An actor needs to commit himself in performance to the words, from moment to moment, and to the phrasing and impulsive rhythms of the writing. He will also, in private rehearsals, try to discover the underlying sequences and compulsions in Hamlet's consciousness without which this long speech cannot be strongly and convincingly shaped. This will involve his unconscious, as well as his conscious mind, because the soliloquy moves towards some of the most unknowable and uncontrollable reactions of mind and body: his awareness of his mother's sexuality and his own in relation to it.

His last and eventually, perhaps, strongest reactions are amazement and revulsion at his mother's 'unrighteous tears' and 'incestuous' second marriage, both feelings heightened by the 'wicked speed' and 'dexterity' with which all has been accomplished. The simple condemnation of line 158 brings the soliloquy to a firm end. Alternatively his speech could be cut off because he hears the sound of persons approaching: in the closed world of the Court (see pp. 22–6, above), what he thinks and feels would be highly dangerous if known by anyone else and so brought to the knowledge of the king.

In performance the actor's imagination has to be full of what is 'gross' and 'unprofitable' in the world, thoughts of his mother's tears and beast-like behaviour, and memories of a god-like and tender father. These clashes of inspiration will be evident in a strong yet varying pulse while, at some moments, the effort to keep a balance between opposing impulses will affect his whole being, body as well as mind. When he begins to think of what he should do, his 'state of man' will suffer 'the nature of an insurrection', as Shakespeare had Brutus in *Julius Caesar* say some twelve months earlier (II.i.67–9). At the start of this soliloquy, the audience sees a young man wishing he were dead; at the end, having been pulled in many directions by scarcely controlled emotions and thoughts, it watches this person as he is forced to be silent and contain within himself all that has threatened his peace of mind.

160–75 Entries and recognitions swiftly and completely alter the mood, tempo, and focus of attention. Exchanges between Hamlet and Horatio are warm, and easily use the short cuts of intimate friendship. Perhaps the good spirits are wholly Hamlet's since these people bring serious and uncertain news. Twice Horatio is asked a simple question and, when he does respond, his answer is evasive and not very convincing.

When Hamlet asks his question a third time (l. 174), he rephrases it and, before Horatio can reply, adds a promise of good fellowship that makes a joking reference to uses of the world that, moments before, had raised no trace of humour. Between these two friends, a deeper contact is established when Horatio answers in the same vein of mockery and antipathy towards the world in which they live.

176–89   Once Horatio has answered his question soberly, against the mood of his jesting, Hamlet speaks more directly of what chiefly concerns him, still making a joke of it but with such brevity that the effect is dark and, probably, fierce. The two friends will now be close to each other physically and at a distance from the third person present.

Hamlet becomes more openly emphatic and satirical and then, speaking directly to his friend, suddenly makes a solemn declaration of absolute and passionate opposition to his mother's wedding (ll. 182–3). After this, as if some obstruction has broken in his mind or he has shuddered and been changed by the force of his passion, very different words follow; first a brief recollection or evocation, and then a simple and unexpected statement: 'methinks I see my father'. Present time is forgotten as imagination and memory take over.

For this moment at least, out of his mother's presence, his father chiefly occupies Hamlet's mind, not so much thoughts of his death but what his memory holds as a living presence. Talk continues uncertainly, with short phrases and simple words that skim over Hamlet's feelings as Horatio withholds the news he has brought for a few more moments. 'I saw him yesternight' brings Hamlet back to the present, both incredulous and amazed (see l. 192).

190–223   After Hamlet's almost speechless 'admiration' [*wonder*], Horatio repeats his news, with 'the King' making it that much clearer. Then calling the other two to join them and with Hamlet's eager encouragement ('God' again marking his deep concern), Horatio starts the story from its beginning, which is not yet known to the theatre audience. Twice Hamlet questions what he is told, the first time drawing Marcellus to add his testimony, but his interrogation stops when Horatio comes to a close. With ' 'Tis very strange' (l. 220), he probably moves further off, lost in the thought that 'troubles' him but that remains, as yet, unspoken. On stage and in the audience, attention will now be fixed on him, waiting for his response.

224–43   After a pause, indicated by the incomplete line 223, and a few non-committal words, Hamlet becomes very practical, his mind moving quickly ahead. His questions are very simple, taking one step at a time, and almost all the answers are equally so. But the number of very short lines suggests that the enquiry goes forward slowly, with everyone aware of its implications. 'I would I had been there' and 'I will watch tonight' are in strong contrast to Hamlet's other responses; the latter, which is also the last, drawing Horatio's endorsement.

244–54   Hamlet is prepared to look into 'hell itself' in order to encounter the 'apparition' (l. 211) and, although he knows he must 'hold [his] tongue' (l. 159), he is also prepared to trust the silence of all three who are present. His mind is racing now: he quickly arranges a meeting and dismisses them all, professing his love toward them. He needs to be alone, as will happen again (see especially, II.ii.54–6 and IV.iv.31). In some unspoken way the others understand this and leave him, rather than waiting for him to make the first move, as decorum in those days would require.

255 to the end   Hamlet's belief that his 'father's spirit' is seeking for him is immediate. Later he will confess that his own 'prophetic soul' had sensed that his uncle, the new king, had murdered his father (I.v.40) but now he speaks only of 'foul play' and longs for the coming night and what will then be disclosed. Eager though he obviously is, he is unable (or afraid) to name what so disturbs his 'soul'.

The couplet that completes the first long scene of the play, declares that evil will always become known to everyone. Perhaps, at this stage, Hamlet believes that he need only wait for that to happen, and has not yet thought of what he should do next. A lot depends on how actively, and up-beat, the actor plays this moment; Hamlet can still be mainly aware of the pain and suffering caused by the 'foul deeds' that will be disclosed.

Act I, scene iii

The audience has been left expecting that, when night comes, Hamlet will meet his 'father's spirit in arms' but now Laertes returns, dressed for his journey to Paris and saying goodbye to his sister, who is a new and unheralded arrival on stage. Unless a spectator knows the story of Hamlet before seeing the play or has read a programme, she will also be an unexpected addition to the persons of the drama. Almost at once they talk about Hamlet in an entirely new light, a view that very soon will be confirmed and amplified by their father: Hamlet has been meeting Ophelia in private and has convinced her of his affection and love. With this information, the tragedy enters territory that has no immediate connection with the world of politics, corruption, re-marriage, and mourning. Here other secrets are kept and other responsibilities apparently forgotten; and here the 'blazes' of sexual desire in a 'young' prince are expected to last only for 'a minute'. And all this the audience hears with Hamlet absent and dramatic focus brought to bear on a young person who says very little. More questions are added to those already raised and they concern not only the play's hero but also the progress of the play itself: how will the two views of Hamlet be reconciled and is Ophelia right to trust him?

1–10   Ophelia enters the play lightly, with her brother ready to leave home and asking her to keep in touch. She seems entirely at ease with him and, in performance, their behaviour and body language are likely to show mutual affection and intimacy. In today's terms, his speech is formal and more than a little pompous but the exchange of line 4 is so easy that it can dispel that impression so far as Ophelia is concerned.

Abruptly changing the subject, 'For Hamlet' (l. 5) will also change the on-stage relationship. When she does reply – or is allowed to do so after 'No more' seems to have wrapped the subject up so far as he is concerned – the negative form of her question can suggest both delicacy of feeling and reserve towards her brother. Ophelia may, however, be so confidently in love with Hamlet that she uses these few words to tease or mock his seriousness. However it is spoken, he brushes her question aside without entering into an argument.

11–28 Laertes continues in such a regular way that the speech often seems to have been prepared for just such an occasion. Perhaps he has culled advice from a book and memorized it; he may have his father's propensity for speaking his mind at length and demonstrating knowledge of the world. What is clear is that Shakespeare has given full scope for showing how a courtier might gossip about 'great' persons and how a self-appointed moralist might judge other people's sexual behaviour – two points of view relevant to many aspects of the play's narrative.

The actor has to choose among several possibilities: 'Perhaps he loves you now' (l. 14) can be either condescending or considerate and loving; 'Carve' (l. 20) is at best callow but could be brutal or betray a lack of concern for a 'weaker' sex.

29–44 With its short phrases, line 33 is the first in which Laertes is tender towards his 'dear sister'. The metaphors of lines 39–42 show a mind full of delicate images taken from the countryside or gardens and, despite the retreat to a standard morality in his concluding couplet, the simpler 'Be wary then' can continue his gentler feelings, as does the advice with which his speech ends.

45–54 Ophelia's first sustained speech is surprisingly controlled, good humoured, knowing about the ways of a 'reckless' world and 'dalliance', and at peace with her 'good' brother. Laertes' reply may be complacent but it can also suggest a level of easy acceptance between the two young people who live under the exacting supervision of Polonius. Both actors will have to discover what happens in this exchange in the light of their entire roles. For him, IV.v.159–60 is a crucial moment to reconcile with his attitude here; for her, 'My brother shall know of it' (IV.v.70) is evidence of a complete trust.

The sound of their father's approach or the opening of a door may cut short longer talk. Q2 places the entry after 'rede' and F after 'fear me not', both arrangements making Laertes' remarks about his father words that he wants him to hear; they are very much in the older man's manner.

55–83   The repetitions and rhythm of line 55 suggest a bustling and overbearing father; so does 'There,' just two lines later. Polonius piles precept on precept at such a steady rate that he is liable to sound insensitive to anybody or anything other than his own prized opinions. Two moments are in contrast: the first, at line 63, starts with a physical and active verb, 'Grapple', as if he has cause to be aware of the effort needed to sustain friendship; the second, the final piece of advice (l. 78), by no means simple to understand or put in practice, is given the strongest emphasis in the long sequence of precepts.

Whatever degree of earnestness the actor gives to Polonius's relationship to his only son, he concludes with a very quick 'blessing' which evokes a one-line response that can be acted impatiently, or even impertinently, rather than 'humbly'. This is another exchange that has to be judged in relation to events and attitudes in Acts IV and V.

It is possible, but not at all easy, to show an underlying bond between all three members of this family over which intransigence and assertion of authority are at a lighter, shallower level of consciousness. Another and surer way of playing this episode is to assume that the deeper feelings that will emerge later are the product of suffering and loss. Or it can be assumed that the two extremes of reaction serve their moments in the narrative and that the actors need not be troubled by consistency. If that is how the play is acted, Ophelia will be by far the most interesting of these persons because both aspects, the heartfelt and the complaisant, are already present so that her very silences here are likely to raise questions or unease in the audience's minds. The lack of first-hand evidence about Hamlet's feelings towards her almost ensures the audience's close attention to the very little that she does say.

84–7   The short exchange between brother and sister contrasts so strongly with their father's long address that, even if quickly played as the need for privacy seems to require, its significance will seem to jump out of focus and catch the audience's attention as it does that of Polonius. Ophelia betters her brother's instruction with an additional promise that implies agreement, if not sympathy, with the brother who has just pressured her into talking about her relationship with Hamlet.

88–104　　Ophelia's careful reply to her father's inquisition guards her own thoughts but is otherwise quite frank. The incomplete line 100 indicates that Polonius is briefly speechless before he brushes aside what she has said and proceeds to a further question that seeks to extract her private thoughts.

The monosyllables of line 104 suggest a slow delivery that is thoughtful in maintaining privacy and yet betrays a sense of wonder. Played in this way, Ophelia assumes that she enjoys Hamlet's whole-hearted affection and respect, but some Ophelias, who have been deceived by a much older and more experienced Hamlet, are here being manipulative of their father. Certainly Ophelia is composed in the face of her father's inquisition, which argues, at least, a strength of mind.

105 to the end　　The incomplete line 111 seems to give Polonius pause before his impatience is made evident in the emphatic, repetitive, and repressive reply. The actor will have difficulty in keeping an audience's sympathy (and, even, its attention) as Polonius warms to his authoritarian theme and assumes that he perfectly understands his daughter's situation.

He is likely to sound more calculating than considerate when he speaks of love as if it were merchandise, a matter of supply and demand (see ll. 121–2). His acceptance of a greater freedom and moral laxity for Hamlet can sound treacherous towards his daughter, not only unfair in assuming male superiority. With the active verb, 'Breathing' (l. 130), his own thoughts can seem to carry him into imaginary and even pleasurable participation in Hamlet's sexual appetite. He concludes with multiple short-phrased commands, as if talking to a disobedient child, not even a 'green girl' (l. 101). Only fear for his daughter's future mitigates such attitudes and, even then, most audiences are likely to be divided in response.

Ophelia's final words in the scene can sound entirely submissive, as if, for the moment at least, she believes her father's view of Hamlet, which coincides with her brother's. At another extreme, they can imply a belief that, whatever she is forced to do, Hamlet will remain faithful in his love for her, as she will be with him. The way she follows her father off stage can be more eloquent than her words, whether expressing her defiance, compliance, or loss of confidence. If she precedes him, she is able to assert her independence or unspoken trust in Hamlet's love. If Polonius were to stay behind for a moment and then hurry to follow, the scene would leave the audience uncertain of the outcome, a response that would seem justified when Hamlet enters immediately afterwards still thinking only of quite other matters.

Act I, scene iv

At the start of the second scene, when the stage was filled with the entire Court, an audience might well have expected that a series of scenes would deal with the political concerns of the 'warlike state' (I.ii.9) with many persons present, but, almost at once, the stage had emptied for Hamlet's first soliloquy and that had led directly into private talk with persons of little political consequence. Two duologues followed in scene iii that involve only three persons on stage. The affairs of Denmark are off stage and may well be out of the audience's mind when Hamlet enters to encounter the Ghost of his father and everything depends on that meeting; the reigning king and queen of Denmark will not be seen again until Act II.

The play has become very small physically and, by that means, encourages a very close attention. Earlier political issues are now developed but in an intensely personal and often sensitive manner, a mode of presentation that will continue throughout the tragedy with only a few larger, crowded, or formal episodes. Most rehearsals of this tragedy involve only the same few actors; many in a company will be called rarely.

1–13   At first, each sentence is short, and, in reaction to the biting cold, the three men may keep moving to keep warm and draw thick outer clothes around them, all of which will establish an unsettled rhythm and mood. Horatio's warning that the Ghost may soon appear is the first longish sentence and comes only after a pause, indicated by the incomplete line 4. Attention is then caught by the '*flourish*' and cannon fire that follow immediately, reminders of that other crowded and ongoing world of the Court. As the sounds die away, Horatio turns to Hamlet, whose answer is the first sustained sentence in the scene (ll. 8–12), which contrasts with all other speeches by the breadth and caustic edge of 'swaggering . . . drains . . . bray out'. Horatio's short questioning response gives Hamlet pause before amplifying what he has said in a yet more condemnatory manner.

14–38 Expressing his opposition more clearly, Hamlet is now more reflective and personal. Lacking any response from the others, he turns from national to personal issues and, without giving names, to 'particular' examples. The many dependent clauses, parentheses, and the emphasis of 'indeed' and 'I say', all show that he is in earnest and possibly – this is the actor's decision – implicating himself in the 'corruption', against which he is left with no defence (see, especially, ll. 25 and 30). He tries to define what is wrong in many ways: 'vicious . . . guilty . . . defect . . . corruption . . . fault . . . evil . . . scandal'. Hamlet is so involved that he does not notice the Ghost's entrance.

This speech will probably veer at times towards soliloquy; if not, Hamlet will have to make sure he holds the attention of his two listeners by speaking directly to them. A number of questions arise from this. Do the three figures keep apart or close together on the otherwise empty stage: are they alert, apprehensive, sharing common feelings or does each react in his own way? Does Marcellus, the one soldier present, keep a continuous guard and, if he does, why does he not give warning of the Ghost's appearance? Are Hamlet's companions uneasy towards him in the strange and ominous circumstances?

39–57 The play's action has made little forward progress while Hamlet talked in general about Danish reputations and human nature but, on the Ghost's entry, everyone, immediately, will be alert. After Horatio's warning, only Hamlet speaks. He must be terrified

because his first words are a prayer, begging for help in conventional
religious terms. He probably steps back in alarm (as illustrations of
this moment depict Garrick and Irving doing; see below, pp. 134 and
138) or he might fall to his knees, perhaps making his response more
specifically Christian by crossing himself.

His recovery is quick because he now addresses the Ghost directly,
but he is not confident, being unsure whether the 'spirit' he addresses
is 'wicked or charitable', heavenly or hellish (ll. 41–2). Hamlet's reference to different explanations of psychic phenomena which were
then current serves the audience's curiosity or possible scepticism
and also establishes once more, at a crucial moment, his instinctive
and well-informed intelligence. He does not, however, doubt the
reality of the Ghost or mention Horatio's earlier opinion that such an
appearance could be the product of an active 'fantasy' (I.i.23): he
knows that everyone present can see the apparition.

When Hamlet calls the Ghost by various names – each one in a
different tone of voice as they touch his feelings differently – none of
them gets a response. His frustration may now be as powerful as his
fear and awe, which are likely to have grown rather than lessened:
night has become 'hideous' and he is shaking like a natural fool or
idiot. He must regain some control to ask the three very simple questions of line 57: it is at this point, and not before, that the Ghost
silently replies. (The stage direction is found in both Q2 and F, and
placed at the same moment.)

58–86 Hamlet is now silent and probably rooted to the spot
because the Ghost continues to beckon him. This behaviour is so
strange that those watching assume he has not got the message or
not even seen the Ghost's gestures. When he does speak (l. 63), it
seems that he has been waiting for some more explicit instruction.
He is still afraid and does not know why; probably for that reason he
still does not move.

To Horatio's reasoned and imaginatively vivid warning of
madness and desperation – important for the audience's understanding as much as for Hamlet's – he makes no reply except, for the third
time, to resolve to 'follow', this time addressing the Ghost with a
respectful 'thee' (l. 79).

After a moment's pause, indicated by the incomplete line 79, Hamlet does move and his companions try to stop him. A violent struggle follows (see 'Hold off your hands. . . . Unhand me, gentlemen') until Hamlet threatens to fight his way free. Probably at this point he draws his sword – it would have been useless against a spirit.

'My fate cries out' is a new committal indicating that Hamlet no longer doubts what to do or has any freedom of action. The three short sentences of line 86 will probably be spoken in a stillness that follows his escape from restraint and, perhaps, from fear. This is the fourth time he says he will follow the Ghost but only now does he do so; probably only now is he capable of doing so.

87 to the end Horatio, the first to speak, fears for Hamlet's safety and sanity, as he had foreseen earlier (see ll. 69–74). The two companions both delay, concerned about what will happen next and the political state of Denmark: this gives the audience time to reflect after the highly dramatic happening while the wider issues of the play again surface into the dialogue.

Before following Hamlet off stage, Horatio, the scholar, puts his trust in the providence of 'Heaven', a hope that Hamlet will voice before facing death in the tragedy's final scene (see V.ii.213–18). For some in the play's early audiences, such a claim would reflect their own way of facing adversity but, in the play, the workings of such a providence can seem wilful or non-existent. Marcellus's response, starting with a negative, encourages an audience to make its own response to the assertion.

Act I, scene v

Even without this scene, Act I would be the longest in the play but its varied action can catch the audience's interest from the start by the Ghost's presence, and hold it in expectation of its return to speak to Hamlet. Now, as two figures enter alone, the audience knows this is about to happen – which it does almost immediately.

Act divisions first appeared in a quarto of 1679, earlier quartos having none, as was usual in printed texts of the time. However, the First Folio marks the beginning of Act II as in modern editions and

thereby gives early authority for the length of Act I. Throughout the
play, the Act divisions of 1679 clearly mark significant stages in the
action and have been retained in all modern editions.

1–9   The ominous word 'revenge' (l. 7) sets the entire play on a new,
single, and firm footing. Hamlet's 'What' marks the shift in his understanding with either an exclamation or a question (the same punctuation mark served both purposes in texts of this time). Even as a
question, its brevity suggests that wonder is likely to be as strong as
foreboding or desire to know more; as an exclamation, the word
would mark a new certainty that his suspicions have been correct
(see l. 40, below).

The identification 'I am thy father's spirit,' spoken by the previously silent spirit between pauses indicated by two incomplete verse-
lines, endorses in private what Hamlet has already assumed. From its
very first words, the Ghost has introduced a new authority to the
dialogue, without ambiguity or hesitation: the word-order is unfamiliar but purposeful; every word is sure and strong, even though
they tell of 'flames' suffered after death in the mysterious (and
disputed) 'prison house' of purgatory (l. 14).

The Protestant England of Shakespeare's day considered purgatory (where the souls of the dead went to expiate for their sins) to be
a popish invention and unbiblical. Many saw it as the Church's device
to extract money by the sale of 'indulgences' that, the priests said,
would reduce the time and suffering in this place of torture situated
between heaven and earth. But the proscribed belief or superstition
persisted; Hamlet does not hesitate to accept that the Ghost's suffering will 'purge away' his 'foul crimes' (ll. 12–13) and, later, his 'imper-
fections' (l. 79). The nature of those crimes remains unspecified but
any great offence would be at odds with Hamlet's several accounts of
his 'noble father'. Earlier, Shakespeare had referred to purgatory in a
clearer and more usual way with regard to Henry IV's specific 'fault'
of killing King Richard: his son had founded two chantries and was
paying 'five hundred poor' to pray for mitigation of his father's
punishment (*Henry V*, IV.i.288–98).

Much remains mysterious in the early exchanges of this
encounter but not the force of the Ghost's call for 'revenge' and its

need to leave before dawn. How far signs of suffering are seen in its face, bearing, or voice is a question left for the actor (or director and designer) to decide: in some recent productions the Ghost is very obviously in agony all the time it is on stage. The one clue in the text comes later when it appears in the Queen's closet and Hamlet tells his mother to 'Look . . . how pale he glares' (III.iv.126).

10–25 The vivid, varied, and almost entirely physical details in the Ghost's account of what Hamlet would suffer if it spoke of purgatory are likely to cause the actor's voice and presence to reflect their sensuous implications. Hamlet's silent response is likely to be no less instinctive and physical; he speaks only after a three-fold call for attention and an appeal to his love for a 'dear father'.

How far 'O God!' (l. 24) is a conscious reference to the Christian God or some other supernatural being is a decision the actor must make. And both actors will have to decide whether this short speech is spoken during a silence, the Ghost waiting before getting to the heart of his message, or whether Hamlet's exclamation is an a-metrical interjection so that the Ghost reaches its conclusion without a pause.

The undoubted feature of this exchange is the highly charged nature of both performances. Before its conclusion, Hamlet knew that Claudius had married his mother within weeks of his father's death but not that his father had been murdered. From this moment, he is called upon to revenge that death.

26–31 As with the earlier 'What', the actor must decide whether Hamlet's 'Murder' is an exclamation or a question, whether it expresses surprise, horror, confirmation, or sympathy. And does it echo the Ghost's words immediately, or after the pause that the incomplete verse-line suggests?

The Ghost's confirmation of its message could scarcely be more measured and authoritative. In reply, Hamlet is amazingly swift, assured, and comprehensive: images of flight and moving (perhaps, too, of cleansing) are linked to 'meditation' or deep thought, and to a conscious 'love' that could be a son's for his father or the passions of sexual desire. All this is in one sentence with syntax and metre that suggest no hesitation and permit almost no pause. Performance will have a sudden and very palpable thrill, in contrast to what has been ominous or horrified. An actor choosing to bring out the more brutal or active aspects of Hamlet will take this speech in his stride, emphasizing his readiness and aptitude for revenge. An actor emphasizing Hamlet's depth of feeling or sense of responsibility will speak it more slowly and thoughtfully.

31–41   The Ghost's reply is measured and reflective, with short phrases and sentences that build towards the heart of his message.

The change of address from 'Hamlet' to 'thou noble youth' (ll. 34 and 38) suggests that Hamlet has responded strongly, in silence, to the rank 'abuse' of everyone's understanding and only then is thought ready to be told that his uncle is the murderer. Hamlet's immediate response might be one of relief because his worst suspicions are now confirmed and strengthened: 'My uncle' would then be an exclamation rather than a question (on the punctuation, see previous notes).

42–59   The Ghost tells its story with a relentless and measured force that encompasses careful detail, wide reflection, precise condemnation, and direct address to Hamlet. Three incomplete verse-lines indicate pauses, during which Hamlet is too wholly involved to say a word. Thoughts of corruption (see ll. 54–7) momentarily deflect the Ghost's attention but the coming dawn draws it back to the narrative.

60–80   The physical effects of the poison are recalled in sensuous detail and with personal involvement (see, especially, ll. 70 and 73) and lead the Ghost back to thoughts of purgatorial punishment and on to the horrified three-fold exclamation of line 80.

Saying 'horrible' three times is such a remarkable change from the rest of the narrative that many editors, from Dr Johnson onwards, have given the line to Hamlet. The emendation is often accepted in performance, chiefly because it involves Hamlet in the narrative and retains his hold on the audience's attention. But all three early texts give these words to the Ghost and, when spoken with a sense of actual and immediate suffering, they can strike like hammer blows on Hamlet's consciousness and, reinforced by his wordless reaction, on the minds and imaginations of everyone in the audience.

81–91 The story finished and time running out, the Ghost gives clearer instructions and is more sensitive to the suffering of his wife – a sensitivity that seems to overflow into the description of the 'glow-worm'. The Ghost's final line may be said while leaving the stage, perhaps seeming to 'fade', as before, on the crowing of a cock (I.ii.217–20). Certainly, 'Remember me' should be spoken in such a way that those two words will haunt Hamlet's mind.

Because the Ghost is later heard from beneath the stage (see l. 149), it has sometimes left by descending through a trapdoor but the effect of that can be laughable. An exit at stage level renders the voice coming from below a more surprising and, possibly, an awesome happening.

92–112 Torn between thoughts of heaven, earth, and hell, his heart pounding and every limb weak, Hamlet struggles in mind and body until the Ghost's last words, 'Remember me,' bring a message he can hold on to and swear to obey.

The act of writing on 'tables' – a notebook of some kind that, at this moment, he will have to produce – is odd and scarcely seems necessary. Some actors take a cue from the 'table' of memory and 'book' of the brain (ll. 98–104) and hold the head to indicate that Hamlet metaphorically 'set[s] it down' in his mind. None of the early texts has a stage direction requiring Hamlet to '*write*'.

112–20 F marks Horatio's entry after he has called out, so that the new dialogue starts from off stage. Equally, Marcellus's 'Illo, ho, ho, my lord' makes more sense if called when Hamlet is not visible to him. No one need enter until after 'Come, bird, come' (l. 116).

'O, wonderful!' may be said in imitation or mockery of the every-day tone of Horatio's question: Hamlet would thereby avoid speaking of the call to revenge that truly occupies his mind and which must be kept secret. Alternatively, the exclamation may sound, to some degree, mad, as if the 'distracted globe' of Hamlet's head (l. 97) were unable to make a better answer. The words *distract* and *distraction* are used in the play with meanings such as mad, frantic, incapable, crazed or crazy (see IV.v.2 and V.ii.223). His previous speech might also be 'distracted' or, at least, wilfully playful.

121–45   Hamlet speaks so oddly that Horatio twice tries to calm him or reason with him before directly criticizing his words as 'wild and whirling'. To some degree Hamlet may be crazed but that impression is more likely to be assumed in order to conceal what he dare not say.

Addressing him by name, Hamlet probably draws Horatio apart to tell him that the Ghost is 'honest' – that being as much as he can safely say – and to caution against more questions; he may also want to show that he is perfectly sane. Then, drawing both 'good friends' together and dropping any semblance of mad behaviour, he asks for help and secrecy (l. 144). Their reply is immediate but for Hamlet too easy: he insists on an oath.

145–82   A run of short, repetitive and urgent speeches is stopped, surprisingly, by the Ghost's 'Swear', from under the stage.

In *Richard II*, swearing on the cross of a sword's hilt is defined as an oath before the Christian God (I.iii.174–82) and so when Hamlet proposes an oath on his sword, he seems to be seeking to sanctify his first steps towards revenge, an undertaking that was against all Christian teaching. Nevertheless, 'Ha, ha, boy . . . truepenny . . . old mole', is jocular, if not crazed, before he addresses the invisible Ghost more solemnly and feelingly as 'perturbèd spirit' (ll. 150, 162 and 182). Just before that, when he warns his friends against hinting that they know something, he uses a clown's trick of imitating the behaviour and speech of others, an ancient theatrical device that raises laughter in many of Shakespeare's comedies.

Although he never questions its authority, Hamlet might well be puzzled by the voice in the 'cellarage', as his companions quite obviously are (see l. 164). An audience unfamiliar with the play, as the earliest ones would have been, would also be surprised and puzzled. In Shakespeare's time, the space under the stage was spoken of as 'hell', and demons were said to 'work' underground and 'shift' their location at will (see ll. 162 and 156). Moreover, the Ghost's repeated and monosyllabic commands are quite unlike his other speeches and previous tardiness in speaking. Much is uncertain in the original texts: they do not indicate why the Ghost should move – does he already feel the torture of purgatory? – or how many times those on stage should swear.

Distracted and puzzled though he may be, Hamlet is also urgent and thoughtful. His oath by St Patrick, keeper of purgatory (l. 136), is quickly passed over but his three calls for an oath are insistent and cover all aspects of the dangerous situation. His friends must swear first not to say what they have 'seen', then not to say what they have 'heard', and, finally, not to hint or show that they know anything about his intentions. The last oath is doubly binding on the hope of both 'grace and mercy' (l. 180).

182 to the end   Wishing peace to the troubled Ghost, Hamlet drops all jocularity and, in performance, can be deeply moved. His words have similarities with 'The rest is silence' at his own death; an audience is unlikely to catch this echo when it comes so much later but it elucidates the text on both occasions and can suggest that Hamlet's desire for peace or 'consummation' (III.i.60–4) is a distinctive element of his innermost being.

After this closer contact with the Ghost with its implied promise of action, Hamlet is more courteous to his friends and newly aware of his own 'poor' state and dependence on 'God'. As they start to leave 'together' – thereby reversing the usual order of precedence – he probably holds back for the concluding couplet, which represents quite another state of mind: one that is deeply personal in accepting a life-time's political responsibility that is not of his choosing. Nowhere in the play so far has he dedicated himself so comprehensively to action: his words hark back to 'My fate cries out' (I.iv.81) and anticipate other significantly placed references to destiny (see III.iv.174–6; IV.iv.36–9; and V.ii.10–11).

After a pause, suggested by the incomplete verse-line, 'Nay' (l. 190) seems to acknowledge that he has not been entirely open with his friends before drawing them 'together' a second time.

ACT II

Act II, scene i

The new scene and new Act start with a jump forward of several weeks and attention is focused on a new character and the absent Laertes. Reynaldo is often omitted in performance because he brings nothing that is necessary to the main action and little is new in the way Polonius deals with him. However, he is present in all three early texts (even the much shorter Q1, where he is called Montano), which shows that the whole scene was thought worth keeping when the detailed instructions to Reynaldo gave audiences a topical impression of a Court under active surveillance and a family subjected to the father's authority. The pains that Polonius takes with regard to his son also serve to keep Laertes in the audience's mind until later, when he will weep for Ophelia's madness and death and seek to revenge his father's death by ruthless and cunning means. The parallels to the watch kept on Hamlet help to clarify the play's main action: much later, before the two young men fight together, Hamlet says that Laertes depicts 'the image' of his own 'cause' (V.ii.77–8).

1–26 The pauses indicated by Reynaldo's incomplete verse-lines and the contrastingly quick response at line 5 suggest that this servant keeps well ahead of Polonius, who at other times is seldom at a loss for words. 'Ay, very well' can be said sarcastically, in mockery of his master's elaborate instruction.

Some actors play the King's counsellor as a laughable old buffer, basing their performance on this scene and Hamlet's description of a 'foolish, prating knave'. Others, who choose to be the astute politician, as described by both Claudius and himself (see II.ii.129–30 and, especially, 153–90), in situations like this will hide his cunning under self-denigration and a show of foolishness. A subtle and skilled Polonius can be seen manipulating a pert and young Reynaldo so that he will be keen and self-confident in seeking out the truth about Laertes. (Compare 'I will find / Where truth is hid . . .'; II.ii.157–9). The competence and, therefore, the status of Polonius is one of the ambiguous features of the tragedy that performance can either resolve or keep in doubt.

27–61 Polonius seems to be caught between allowing his son a 'fiery mind' in sexual matters and demanding some of the restraint that he expects his daughter to maintain. The length at which this dilemma is explored and the obvious hesitation or failure to find the right word, which causes a movement from verse into prose, can either show a subtle Polonius making sure that Reynaldo understands the delicacy of the matter or one out of his depth as a father, floundering and losing the thread of what he is saying.

62–74 Much depends on how earnestly Polonius explains the necessity of using 'falsehood' or how self-satisfied he is at the prospect of catching the 'carp of truth'. On one hand, he can appear over-ingenious or complacent; on the other, genuinely anxious, prudently insistent, or heartless and unsympathetic.

Short lines indicate an awkward end to the interview, whichever way it is played. Ambiguities remain, notably in 'let him ply his music': is this a kindness to his son or a means of taking away any suspicion that Reynaldo is a spy?

74–86 Although she is seeking help from her father, who has previously shown her no sympathy, Ophelia probably enters in the greatest possible haste. Her first frightened words alarm him: she may have run into his arms or stopped still to master her 'affrighted' feelings. After a pause, she regains sufficient control to give an account of Hamlet from the beginning of their latest encounter. One detail at a time, she depicts the man with whom she had spent hours in loving and private talk as one who is unapproachable, wordless and 'piteous' (l. 82). While Polonius jumps to the conclusion that he is mad for love of his daughter – as Ophelia fears that he is – an audience, remembering that Hamlet planned to 'put an antic disposition on' (I.v.172), may doubt whether this is true.

87–100 Lines 91 and 96 may both be spoken as a pair of incomplete verse-lines, a short silence between each sentence as Ophelia remembers and then demonstrates how Hamlet had touched and made contact with her (see 'thus', ll. 89 and 93). This enactment will leave her at a distance from her father.

In Ophelia's words and actions, Hamlet has returned to the play for the first time since seeing his father's ghost, and his involvement with Ophelia is now an established fact. Much, however, remains uncertain because all the signs of madness could be a means of diverting attention and a cover for his resolve to murder the king. This had been Hamblet's reason for pretending to be mad in the ancient saga that was Shakespeare's source (see p. 14, above).

101 to the end   Polonius is decisive and confident enough to support his action with a general reflection in his more usual manner. 'I am sorry' (l. 106) starts a new line of thought that makes him question Ophelia and then to find fault with his own 'judgement' and 'jealousy'. Those thoughts lead once again to a general reflection, as if, even now, he cares more about his own 'opinions' (l. 115) than his daughter.

Ophelia becomes very conspicuously silent although Polonius involves her in his plan of action from his very first words (l. 101). 'That hath made him mad' (l. 110) may be said with self-satisfied assurance but, however spoken, these words will have a crushing effect on Ophelia, who, unwillingly, had followed her father's instructions. 'Come,' the last word in the scene, is his third command: it could be spoken gently and sympathetically, or apologetically after his admission of error; its brevity is, perhaps, more suitable for an unfeeling and repressive attitude to his daughter.

If Ophelia hesitates before leaving with Polonius or if she quickly goes out before him, she will draw all eyes of the audience, which has been kept waiting for her response. She has no words to speak but, with this preparation, her smallest reaction would be noticed. Perhaps she weeps uncontrollably before leaving the stage, or stays behind and then leaves in an opposite direction, occupied with her own thoughts of what she believes to be a mutual and courageous love. In the next scene, Polonius goes alone to the King, as if Ophelia's behaviour has led to second thoughts about the most effective approach.

Act II, scene ii

By far the longest scene in the play, this is also the one in which Hamlet speaks his mind most freely to his 'excellent good' friends 'of so young days brought up with him' (ll. 224 and 11) and to the actors, whom he knows well, their leader being his 'old friend' (l. 421). At times he seems to speak his innermost thoughts but intimacy is varied with deep suspicion, pretended madness, genuine passion and, perhaps, some sign of actual madness. The scene ends with a soliloquy that is often the most violent in performance and, in its concluding lines, the most deliberate and purposeful.

1–18 Although located in 'the lobby' at line 161, the '*Flourish*' (from Q2) and the reception of ambassadors suggest a more formal setting, possibly a Council chamber. In some recent productions the King and Queen have sat at a table as if ready to conduct an interview.

19–32 Rosencrantz and Guildenstern are sometimes played to comic effect as two indistinguishable and pliable young men but, from the first, their speeches suggest a difference that can become progressively clear in performance. Here Rosencrantz, somewhat tactlessly, draws attention to the mixture of 'entreaty' and 'command' in what the King has said, while Guildenstern, more knowingly, emphasizes their compliance by adding that their obedience is 'freely' given.

33–9 The reversed order of address in the Queen's thanks is likely to raise a laugh in performance, sometimes intentionally in order to lessen a tension that arose when Hamlet's friends accepted the role of spies. The more urgent 'beseech . . . instantly . . . Ay, amen' reveal a deeper concern. Claudius adds nothing but may move to reassure her or prevent more being said: he knows that his new wife 'Lives almost by [her son's] looks' (IV.vii.11–12).

40–53 As a trusted counsellor, Polonius has immediate and privileged access to the royal presence. Having introduced official business, he takes the further and unusual step of raising a private matter, excusing his presumption. In *The Prince*, Machiavelli warned a ruler to suspect any minister or courtier who offered advice or raised any subject without first being asked to do so.

54–8   Claudius introduces a more personal note with 'my dear Gertrude', but her reply is terse, acknowledging the consequences of her own haste. The moment is awkward: Claudius is then even more terse as if, unwittingly (see III.iv.31), she has reminded her husband of his own more certain and more appalling guilt (see III.iii.36–9).

58–85   The official business is smoothly introduced, handled with a well marshalled and probably rehearsed speech, and then graciously completed by the King. Although the episode deals with threats of war and long-held rivalries, its effect in performance is calming, both by its well controlled progress and by the shift of attention from what concerns the principal persons present at a deep and personal level.

85–105   Polonius's preamble is often played for laughs, either at his expense or as if he is mocking his own formality and loquacity. It can, however, be the expression of considerable unease before saying, bluntly, 'Your noble son is mad' (l. 92), words that could be considered treasonous. Certainly, an apology follows and, perhaps, a further expression of embarrassment with 'But let that go.' The Queen's rejoinder can sound tart but could, alternatively, be sympathetic and an encouragement to continue.

Polonius becomes still more self-conscious and, perhaps, more laughable as he prepares to speak of Hamlet's love for his daughter and therefore of his own close involvement with the monarch's most private and dynastic concerns. In a time of autocratic royal rule, he is in great danger, as is his daughter. Some in the audience may realize that he has changed his mind, as if he had been afraid to bring Ophelia in person before the King (see II.i.117–20).

106–28   Polonius starts circumspectly by guarding himself and Ophelia against the charge of presumption or dynastic ambition. Even if his speech is played for laughs, he is clearly unsure of himself, asking for close attention ('mark') and leaving his hearers to interpret the very clear message of what he is about to read.

Uncertainty continues, because Polonius's comments on Hamlet's phrases can be comically self-important or finicky but they could also be a crafty avoidance of more serious comment, which leaves the King and Queen to 'surmise' (l. 108) the consequences.

The letter also raises major questions for the actor of Hamlet. When was it written? Was it intended as part of his feigned madness or does it represent his true feelings as well as he was able? What effect did he believe it would have on Ophelia? Are its excessive and repetitive phrases a sign of worship (see 'idol', l. 109), sensuality (see 'fire', l. 115), or, as Polonius thinks, a mind infatuated to the point of madness? At this point in the play, the audience has heard no evidence from Hamlet's own lips, only Ophelia's account of his 'tenders' and 'holy vows' (I.iii.99–114); it has, however, seen recent signs of mental and physical suffering (see II.i.75–100). As Polonius asks of the King and Queen, 'what might [they] think' (ll. 131–9) of both Ophelia and Hamlet? And how should both actors play their roles at this stage of the play? Is fear or love dominant in Ophelia? Does Ophelia affect all of Hamlet's being, as she believes (see II.i.94–6)?

How Polonius reads the letter will affect his hearers on stage and in the audience. Does he very obviously omit a more sensuous passage at line 96? As he proceeds, his comments stop and some actors choose to make him increasingly committed to the sentiments he expresses, if only to keep or gain close attention. In other performances, Polonius makes a mockery of everything he reads and emphasizes every phrase he considers insane. Almost certainly, an audience will become still more concerned to know what Hamlet thinks in what he later calls his 'heart's core' (III.ii.83). Perhaps Hamlet himself does not know his own mind at this stage of the play: see 'I did love you once. . . . I loved you not' (III.i.115–19).

128–51 Before supplying the further evidence that Claudius demands, Polonius puts himself on the line. Perhaps he moves closer or changes his tone of voice before speaking of 'this hot love', as if his earlier evidence has been accepted. Anxiety remains, however, through a series of questions in which he pointedly includes Hamlet's mother (l. 135). He seeks to protect himself by stressing the propriety of his handling of the matter and his daughter's subsequent rejection

of Hamlet's advances. Through a series of similar phrases – 'then . . .
thence . . . thence . . .' – he defends himself by stressing that Hamlet's
'madness' had only gradually become apparent.

Listening to Polonius, the King and Queen usually remain sitting
in the chairs or thrones in which they have given audience to
Rosencrantz and Guildenstern and the Ambassadors. With a less
formal arrangement at a long table, Polonius might be signalled
(perhaps at l. 135) to sit with them across the table for his long, somewhat more relaxed speech.

151–70 The simply worded and incomplete verse-line with which
Gertrude gives her opinion (l. 152) suggests that she is still caught up
with the doubts and guilt expressed earlier (ll. 56–7). With 'Take this
from this,' Polonius stakes his life on his judgement and so breaks a
potential deadlock: he immediately puts forward his plan to use
Ophelia to trap Hamlet.

Neither King nor Queen remarks on this treatment of Ophelia,
which some in the audience may consider more proper to 'a farm and
carters' (l.167) than a father and his daughter. Although Gertrude
shows obvious sympathy with the 'poor wretch', her son, neither she
nor Claudius takes notice of the aggressive connotations of 'I'll board
him presently' (1. 170). The episode finishes rapidly, in contrast to the
slow entry of Hamlet, who is reading 'sadly' (l. 168).

To walk around a palace reading a book is very strange behaviour
and should probably be taken as an 'antic disposition' which Hamlet
has assumed to hide his secret intention to revenge his father's
murder; it would also be a way of keeping watch on what is happening at Court.

171–86 Q1 places 'To be or not to be' (III.i.56ff.) here, unlike the
other two early texts. Perhaps Shakespeare's first thought was to
emphasize Hamlet's suicidal melancholy when he returns to the
stage after his energetic conclusion to the first Act. The rapidity with
which greetings turn to a 'mad' attack on Polonius takes the narrative
forward more strongly and the question about his daughter develops
the audience's curiosity about Hamlet's relationship to Ophelia (see
comment on ll. 106–28).

For Shakespeare's contemporaries, Hamlet speaking in prose was another exceptional feature of this entry. Marlowe had also used prose for his tragic hero in *Dr Faustus* when conjuring spirits or almost powerless before his death, and elsewhere for true madness: in this scene, Hamlet is in his right mind and not always acting madness.

The incongruity of calling Polonius a 'fishmonger' (l. 174) nearly always raises a laugh, even though its meaning may not be grasped. A disreputable quibble on 'fleshmonger' is comparatively easy to suggest but not the meanings, at one time current, of *bawd* or *breeder of many libidinous women* (see Arden edition, series 2). The latter would lead on to the talk of maggots breeding and so to Polonius's daughter (ll. 181–2). When the actor suits action to these meanings, Hamlet becomes a gross caricature of lust and shameless insolence; to Polonius he seems 'far gone' (l. 189), but not beyond belief.

187–92   The first of three passages spoken aside, to himself or to the theatre audience, draws attention to Polonius's predicament. It can express a genuine concern for Hamlet until it awakens an unexpected memory of his own suffering in 'youth'; alternatively, Polonius remains entirely absorbed in his attempt to keep pace with the thoughts of the apparent madman. While Polonius talks, Hamlet sometimes continues to read, or pretends to do so.

192–204   Hamlet may play with 'words' to devalue them in comparison with his own thoughts or to avoid more interrogation, but most actors speak of 'old men' in open mockery of Polonius, who may, indeed, end up going 'backward' (l. 204) as, 'like a crab', he moves sideways to escape contact.

205–21   By drawing attention to 'method' (l. 206) in Hamlet's pretended madness, Polonius encourages an audience that has laughed at Hamlet's play-acting to be aware of another level in his consciousness. Those spectators who have caught an element of self-criticism in 'Words, words, words' (l. 193), may now sense an instinctive death-wish as he plays with thoughts of his 'grave' and the taking of 'life' (ll. 215–17).

Some actors, however, will suggest that Hamlet is, indeed, being drawn 'from th'understanding of himself' (ll. 8–9, above) and in danger of becoming the madman he pretends to be. Certainly, he shows volatility and relish in the encounter. The outright dismissal in 'These tedious old fools' can be unnecessarily cruel, an instinctive expression of frustration, or an occasion for bitter laughter. In effect, Hamlet tantalizes Polonius and the audience so that they are uncertain how to take him.

The brevity of the exchange between Polonius and Rosencrantz and Guildenstern can suggest he is glad to escape. 'There' indicates that Hamlet is now some distance away, occupied with his own thoughts.

222–37 Hamlet's affectionate greeting of his friends is marked by a return to the usual staple of verse. But their replies are not so confident and, with more adventurous wordplay, the dialogue returns to prose, as in Hamlet's previous 'mad' encounter. Occasionally, throughout his ensuing talk with Rosencrantz and Guildenstern, the actor and theatre audience may be unsure whether Hamlet is acting madness or not, to what extent his words are instinctive and involuntary, deeply considered and probing, or tentative. By allowing considerable time for this meeting, Shakespeare was able to show the wide range of Hamlet's thoughts and their conflicting impulses, while demonstrating the surveillance under which he lived, and, with the arrival of the Players, the heroic and mythical dimensions of the play's action.

By talk of 'Fortune' (l. 229), Guildenstern may be trying to cue Hamlet to say what 'afflicts him' (ll. 114–17) but, taking up the topic, he uses it to question him: 'What news?' (l. 235). Guildenstern has no ready answer, probably aware of the implications. Rosencrantz intervenes with a very general and ironic response. The mood has quickly grown uneasy.

238–64 Hamlet turns what Rosencrantz has said to thoughts of the end of the world and its 'doom' or 'true' judgement and then directly faces and questions both his 'good friends' about their intentions. Almost certainly he has suspected a trap. His reference to

Denmark as a 'prison' can be intended as a sign of his pretended madness and also as a challenge that requires an answer: possibly it says more than Hamlet intended of his true state of mind. Guildenstern is quick to question the word, once more taking the lead.

As the verbal sparing with his two friends seems about to break down in misunderstandings (ll. 242–4), Hamlet turns to scepticism: 'there is nothing either good or bad but thinking makes it so' is close to the phrasing of Montaigne's *Essays* (see above, pp. 18–19). When Rosencrantz tries to turn this to more particular matters, as Hamlet had done, 'O God' (l. 253) seems to indicate a sudden impulse in reply, perhaps with a new awareness that his own mind is full of 'infinite' possibilities and personal nightmares. After Guildenstern tries to pin him down, the mood changes yet again and Hamlet starts to move off and seek other company at Court, dismissing any 'reason' in what he has said.

265–92 As Rosencrantz and Guildenstern revert to customary politeness, Hamlet changes tack yet again, remembering a friendship that is 'dear' (l. 273) and 'beaten' like a well trod path (l. 269) but concluding with a series of short and direct questions (ll. 274–5). When his friends are alternately silent and evasive, Hamlet voices his suspicion, which has now become a certainty (see l. 281). Answered again with prevarication, he persists with his question by appealing to the 'rites of fellowship', their 'ever-preserved love' and a still dearer 'charge' than friendship. He may now be speaking with irony or in desperation.

The '*aside*' marked for Hamlet (l. 290), like many similar stage directions, is not in any of the original texts but the addition of later editors. The meeting is at such an impasse that nothing is likely to be hidden. After whatever pause or silence is called for in each performance, Guildenstern takes the lead once more and confesses to what Hamlet, by now, knows well enough: 'we were sent for'.

Without the control and impetus of verse and when the audience knows very well what is at risk, the breakdown of dialogue can have a startling effect by the most ordinary means of hesitation, avoidance, stumbling, repetition and so forth.

293–310   Hamlet passes over the palpable embarrassment of his erst-
while friends with a confession of melancholy – a fashionable pose in
Shakespeare's day to which he often referred around the turn of the
century (see, for example, *As You Like It*, IV.i.3–9). He probably offers it
as an alternative to madness, which would similarly explain his solitariness and disguise his determination to take revenge. In effect he is
taunting and playing with the King's spies and yet he speaks with such
fluency and fervour that melancholy and thwarted idealism may well
seem an essential part of his nature. Each actor will 'tune' this remarkable speech differently, emphasizing 'either [the] good or bad' (l.249),
and, in doing so, set his individual mark on the role.

311–67   Talk is now more frank than before and, with news of the
Players, Hamlet responds as if their performance will satisfy every
element of his 'dreaming' or idealism, each player acting perfectly.
Later, Rosencrantz speaks of a 'kind of joy' in him when hearing of
their approach (III.i.18).

   What follows is in a different key: topical in Shakespeare's
London, detailed in regard to theatre management and reputation,
and driven forward by Hamlet's questions. Today scholarly notes are
needed to explicate much of what is said and the passage is usually
heavily cut in performance. Enough will be kept for Hamlet to bring
the subject to a close with thoughts of his father and uncle, together
with allusion to what is 'more than natural' – or 'rotten' (I.iv.90) – in
the state of Denmark and calls him to take revenge.

368–94   An off-stage trumpet announcing the Players cuts off
further talk. Distrust seems to evaporate as Hamlet welcomes his two
friends once more. He invites them closer to shake hands and, in a
self-deprecating joking manner, sets their minds at rest with regard
to his 'madness'. On Polonius's entry he takes them further into his
confidence by mocking the old counsellor for being childish and
telling them what they already know as if it were 'news' (ll. 388–9).
The energy and variety in what Hamlet says invite demonstrative
physical performance.

395–401   Polonius faces Hamlet's high-spirited mockery or, as he
would take it, his antic madness with what we would call literary

criticism. The contest can be one-sided, either way: Polonius can firmly and regularly complete his catalogue of dramatic genres as a way of reproving and so calming Hamlet. He, on the other hand, can mercilessly respond to the old man with laughter, in which his companions join.

401–19   Taking a hint from 'the only men', Hamlet changes tack and fixes attention on Polonius. With the words of a popular ballad, he identifies him as the Old Testament father who, in return for victory in battle, made an oath to God that he would sacrifice the first living creature he encountered afterwards: it was his virgin daughter.

Hamlet may imitate madmen in the drama of the time, who would stare and fix their eyes on the person their fantasy identified as their victim or some famous person (see, for example, *Julius Caesar*, IV.iii.40 and *King Lear*, IV.v.108).

A major question is whether the 'mad' Hamlet is rebuking Polonius for misusing his daughter or warning him that she is in danger of dying. He may be glad that the Players' arrival allows him to lighten the mood.

420–31   The warmth and individual greetings of Hamlet's welcome provide a marked change of mood as he moves among the actors. Luggage, in the form of costume hampers and stage properties, will often be brought on stage and individual players give improvised responses to Hamlet, using the 'liberty' of performance (l. 400). The stage is quickly and variously alive until Hamlet calls for a speech. The opportunity to see a perfected performance at once attracts him; like a 'falconer' (l. 428), he will be alert and purposeful, perhaps 'passionate' like the speech he wants to hear.

Since Polonius entered, Hamlet has been so 'full of changes' (*King Lear*, I.i.279), he may well seem mad when he does not intend to be so.

432–49   The choice demanded by the Player does not take Hamlet unawares but he delays giving his answer to warn that his choice is not popular: it was acted 'not above once' and the 'excellent' play had pleased only a few people. Amazingly, however, it has so lived in Hamlet's memory that, after a false start, he can speak a dozen lines of it by heart: among many other small details in the play-text, this marks Hamlet as a deeply private person with a sharply focused and retentive mind.

As every one stands around waiting for Hamlet to name the play, he delivers a discriminating account of its dramatic structure and theatrical style, as if proving his critical credentials. Words come freely, as if he has often thought about this subject, and his 'judgements' are expressed antithetically: both 'digested' and 'set down'; as much 'modesty as cunning . . . as wholesome as sweet . . . more handsome than fine'; 'sallets' are opposed to 'matter', 'affectation' to 'honest method'. Hamlet is not speaking about any 'necessary question' of the play but his thoughts about another play reveal more about the nature of his mind. Later, in talking to the players, he will return to the same subject as he considers how *The Murder of Gonzago* will be performed (see III.ii.1–53). Actors of Hamlet will often take these two discourses as encouragement to make him constantly aware of the effect of what he says and able to shape his speeches with both 'modesty' and 'cunning'. This complicates the earlier (and repeated) distinction between 'actions that a man might play' and 'that within which passes show' (I.ii.83–6). Here, the play's story is put on hold in order to show Hamlet as an intellectual who is cunning and observant, as well as a secretive man of passion and action.

450–62 By remembering and speaking this speech Hamlet is shown to be committed to the thoughts of a tiger-like – that is how Hamlet thinks of him at first (see l. 448) – and 'hellish' young soldier who revenges the abduction of another man's wife. He stops performing when he comes to speak of the helpless father, Priam. The style of the speech is also significant as preparation for the later play-within-the-play and as a demonstration of how far Hamlet's imagination can go beyond the staple of his own words, in powerful but less subtle ways.

As he speaks the speech, Hamlet stands apart from everyone else on stage. Polonius's comment (especially if compared with his remarks on the First Player's performance, ll. 517–18) suggests that Hamlet has held back from a fully physical or passionate performance: he is not yet ready to commit to action.

463–516   When the First Player takes over from Hamlet, the drama watched by the theatre audience changes, as if with a shift of gear. Attention is focused on one man while his imagination conjures up visions of a vast battlefield and the clash of two dynasties in which a bloodied warrior kills a defenceless and aged king while his wife, the mother of his children, cries out to inscrutable gods.

The ornate, sensuous and archaic style of this speech, indebted to Virgil and Marlowe, together with its evocation of the mythical Trojan war, distance the on-stage drama further from the lives of its theatre audience and, for its duration, obscure the presence of the hero and other persons of *The Tragedy of Hamlet*. The transportation is so thoroughly effected that it can awaken expectation that a similar 'rage' (l. 470) will strike widely and terribly before the action of the main play concludes.

The role of First Player is usually given to an actor of long experience and innate authority on stage or, sometimes, to one in his prime, to ensure an exceptional force for the demanding speech.

496–502   The break in the First Player's performance while comments are made probably occurs during one of its several pauses. The others, indicated by incomplete verse-lines, may strike even deeper in the consciousness of its on-stage audience: Pyrrhus unable to act while the heavens threaten disaster; and his killing of the king (ll. 480 and 490). A physical or audible reaction from Hamlet may draw attention in the theatre away from the Player.

Incidentally, the exchange between Hamlet and Polonius defines their relationship without the complication of pretended madness.

517–32   When Polonius breaks the silence that follows the Player's performance, Hamlet and, almost certainly, the theatre audience will be held in silence by the imagined reality of cruelty and terror. Ignoring him, Hamlet takes charge of the situation, promising to hear what remains of the same speech. He is short with Polonius, who is less than generous to the Player, and corrects 'Come, sirs' by calling them 'friends', as he did in his first greeting (ll. 532 and 421).

533–46   Already Hamlet has a new and complete plan in his mind and draws the first Player aside to gain his assistance. When protecting Polonius from mockery he will seem at ease with both parties, confident and, perhaps, laughing. With a few courteous words to his 'good friends', his fellow students, he makes sure he is 'alone'.

547–54   As Act II draws to a close, Hamlet has been on stage continuously for the longest time so far, an exposure that will not be equalled until the tragedy's concluding scenes. Now, at last, speaking to himself or to the audience, he starts by voicing amazement and shame at his inaction and lack of 'passion' and physical response to the murder of his father.

555–79   As before (ll. 500–1), Hecuba, the Queen-mother, halts forward movement before Hamlet's thoughts take a wider view of his predicament, one that involves other people – 'the guilty . . . free . . . [and] ignorant'. Returning to himself at line 563, within five lines he is asking if cowardice holds him back from action, now imagined in terms of tearing the intestines from his enemy. In a short torrent of words – in contrast to his reaction to Hecuba – he denounces Claudius many ways and then, with a cry, calls in one word for 'vengeance', at which point the actor may well shudder or weep with frustration as he falls silent.

580–5   Returning to himself, after the incomplete verse-line, he is no longer an actor, but an 'ass' and, almost immediately, a 'whore' – a reaction made more pointed in 'stallion' [*male prostitute*] of Q1 and F than in 'scullion' [*kitchen menial*] of Q2. Sexual revulsion will become more strongly expressed in later scenes where he is alone with Ophelia, at the play, with his mother and, briefly and bitterly, in the final encounters (see III.i.111–22; III.ii.121–36; III.iv.65–95; and V.ii.209–20 and 319–20).

586 to the end   Having already called for *The Murder of Gonzago* and proposed writing an additional speech, Hamlet is now so caught up in the plan that he articulates how it will work even though it seems to be an entirely new idea at this moment (see ll. 592–4).

As he sees the 'course' ahead, Hamlet's mind is more open than before about the nature of the Ghost: it might come from heaven or hell, or it could be the product of his own 'melancholy'. But the soliloquy and the long scene finish with a decisive couplet in which he sees himself as a successful hunter and as an investigator or judge with the means to penetrate behind appearances. As he leaves the stage, the audience knows that the play's action is poised to take a major and decisive step forward.

ACT III

Two meetings that have been long delayed bring Hamlet alone with Ophelia and then with his mother: between them comes a second full-scale Court scene in which the actors perform their play until Claudius stops them and leaves the stage. All three crucial events draw the audience's closest attention as passions flare and words are unable to express all that is involved. After the play Hamlet is left in no doubt about his father's murder but on his way to his mother's closet he does not take an opportunity to kill Claudius. After the narrow focus of Act II, the narrative's context has widened again and, before its close, the Act has several surprising outcomes: Hamlet has killed Polonius; he is estranged from Ophelia whom he has insulted; the Ghost has returned in a new form; and, having made peace with his mother, Hamlet leaves her to be torn by 'sighs' and 'profound heaves' (IV.i.1).

Act III, scene i

After Hamlet's passionate and, finally, decisive soliloquy, the new Act starts simply and coolly, with the King and Queen interviewing Rosencrantz and Guildenstern, but, unlike the similar occasion in Act II, scene ii, Ophelia is also present, a silent witness.

1–28 According to Q2 and F, '*Lords*' are in attendance, rather than '*attendants*' as at the start of Act II, scene ii. However, these supernumeraries have been given nothing to say or do, nor is any exit marked for them. Editors often omit them, making this a private interview rather than a public audience. Perhaps the Lords are present in good texts because Shakespeare wanted to demonstrate the political consequences of Hamlet's assumed madness but did not develop the idea. Even their silent presence ensures that the interview is a public event, with underlying anxieties kept under restraint.

As Rosencrantz and Guildenstern respond they can either seem eager to report on their friend or careful to do so accurately and with enough detail to show they have done their work thoroughly. Again Guildenstern is the second to speak and with greater precision than his fellow (see II.ii.29–32 and 38–9, etc.), the difference between them accentuating their need to connive with authority.

Two incomplete verse-lines indicate hesitations, marking a greater delicacy after the Queen's interventions. A third and fourth precede the King's approval of the Players' performance and his new instructions to the two spies. These breaks in the verse, together with the young men's speedy departure, suggest an unspoken uneasiness from the start of this interview.

28–42   Claudius now reveals his intention of becoming a spy himself, together with Polonius. His words are carefully chosen: '*Sweet* Gertrude . . . *closely* sent . . . *lawful* espials'. In response Gertrude says very little but takes time to speak gently and hopefully to Ophelia, who has been standing, silent and ignored, throughout these proceedings, which concern her closely. Her brief reply to the Queen and the body language of both women can establish a positive understanding and sympathy between them. Alternatively, Ophelia may say little because she is wholly concerned with Hamlet's well-being and apprehensive about being used to entrap him. Either way, dramatic focus will be concentrated upon a narrative line that cannot be openly presented.

43–55   If antithetical speech, careful wording and hesitations have not already suggested Claudius's hidden guilt, this 'heavy burden' is revealed in the aside that follows the confident duplicity of Polonius in handling his daughter. Whether spoken slowly with painful emphasis or blurted out, as if trying to lance 'the quick o'th'ulcer'

(IV.vii.122), it is the first of a sequence of similar disclosures (see
III.iii.36–72 and 97–8; IV.i.45, IV.iii.68–70).

Ophelia may either continue to 'walk', reading the book (as
Hamlet had done; see II.ii.168), or walk to a place where she can kneel
as if she were following a religious 'exercise' described in a devotional
book. Polonius's words offer her no sympathy or respect; however,
he immediately thinks of the 'devil himself', as if he knows the wrong
he has done.

However painful the situation for Ophelia and, possibly, for
Claudius and Polonius, the audience's attention is swiftly taken away
by Hamlet's entry.

56–82   Taking 'arms against' his troubles holds Hamlet's attention
only for a moment before he thinks repeatedly of dying, first as a
peaceful consummation and then as entry to a dream-like afterlife.
The thought that those dreams could be unbearable nightmares leads
him back to the 'fardels' [*burdens*] of everyday living and a fear of
death. He neither thinks of his father's ghost when he says no 'traveller returns' from death nor does he remember his promise to
revenge, which would be reason enough to choose life rather than
death. He is at a low point in his journey through the play: from the
first words of the soliloquy he sees himself caught between two
possible decisions; failing to decide between them, he is puzzled in
his will, his body feels the strain, and his imagination dreads the
coming of death.

A very different way of playing this entry is for Hamlet to know he
is being watched, having been 'sent for' (l. 29), as Rosencrantz and
Guildenstern had been (II.ii.281 and 292). The soliloquy then becomes
a smokescreen to hide his deepest thoughts and feelings while giving
vent to other troubles and uncertainties.

83–92   When he thinks of himself as a 'coward', as he did in the
previous soliloquy (II.ii.568), Hamlet is reminded of his great 'enterprise' and the need for 'action'. His mood and bearing change and,
being more alert, he at last notices Ophelia. He stops to address her
with courtesy and respect before thinking – it seems instinctively – of
his own sins. *Nymph* and *orisons* are both, however, fanciful and

archaic words and may be intended to show that Hamlet is only acting the respect or that he speaks with an edge of irony.

The meeting, so long delayed, releases feelings very different from any that could have been accompanied by 'almost all the holy vows of heaven' (I.iii.110–14). His mother's 'frailty' (I.ii.146) seems to have destroyed Hamlet's belief in any woman's 'honesty' (ll. 107–15) and can affect his response from the moment he catches sight of Ophelia. When he speaks of his own 'sins' (l. 90), earlier feelings may have gone beyond recall.

Influenced by what she has just heard from Claudius and from Hamlet's student friends, Ophelia's respectful reply can be both loving and fearful. A hint of reproach may be heard in the allusion to his absence for 'many a day'.

As the two declared lovers become fully aware of each other's presence, Hamlet's stumbling response indicates that his strongest and most immediate sensations lie beyond the reach of words. The repetition of 'well' is only in F and may be an unauthorized addition (perhaps recording an actor's way of marking the crucial moment); the single 'well' of Q2 could be a conscious refusal to say more or an admission that he is unable to say more.

How the subsequent meeting is played depends on other factors of great importance that are not answered one way or another in any of the texts. Has Ophelia heard that the King and her father will be secretly spying on them? Does Ophelia believe that Hamlet is mad, as she earlier feared (see II.i.85–6)? At some stage is Hamlet pretending to be mad? Does he already know that he is 'be-netted round with villainies' (V.ii.29) or does he only suspect or sense that Ophelia is being used as a trap? With much to consider as they meet each other on stage for the first time, the actors are likely to perform warily: this is a physical, sensual, sexual, and highly nervous event, as well as a verbal exchange. The audience, which has been kept waiting for this meeting, is likely to watch closely.

93–162 The preceding soliloquy is now the most famous feature of the tragedy, having currency far beyond the bounds of theatre, but it is neither so innovative nor, in performance, so startling as the ensuing duologue. The verbal style, content, and emotional development of the soliloquy had been foreshadowed in earlier plays and, in this play, Hamlet had longed for death in his first soliloquy (see I.ii.129–37) and resolved on action in his second (see II.ii.592–603). In contrast this meeting between two lovers is unprecedented: much of it is in prose, with many contradictions, repetitions, and silences; it is rived by misunderstandings and driven by feelings of revulsion as well as love and tenderness. The audience's attention is taken beneath conscious thought and what can be openly spoken or enacted.

At the end of this encounter, Hamlet leaves alone, having said he has been made mad as if it were no longer a pretence, while Ophelia, steadfast in admiration and love, remains on stage, grieving for Hamlet and herself.

93–102 A silence precedes Ophelia's rejoinder as she offers his remembrances back, as her father had told her, but adding that she had long wanted to do so. When he denies giving these gifts or anything else, she pauses a second time before contradicting him and, again, presses him to take the remembrances. By retaining verse for this difficult opening exchange, Shakespeare was able to indicate and, to some extent, control its pauses.

103–20 Hamlet's two unanswered and unanswerable questions lead to the baffling statement of lines 107–8 and on, through her puzzled question and his 'paradox', to a confession of love that, almost at once, is contradicted. Ophelia's replies are honest and modest; the last, surely, stricken with regret and pain (l. 120). Perhaps she sinks to the ground or breaks away from her interrogator. She may well be in tears.

121–34 Twice sending her to a nunnery and accusing himself of degrading and multiple 'offences', Hamlet renders Ophelia speech-less until the sudden 'Where's your father?' If she has not heard the secret talk between Polonius and Claudius (at ll. 28–37 and 43–55), she may reply as she thinks would be the case. If she has heard everything, she is lying for one of several possible reasons: not knowing what else to say, the truth being so complex and the King such a threat to Hamlet; or being so frightened by what she has just heard, she must find some way of stopping further inquisition; or being so weakened and stressed, she says what she thinks her father would wish.

Hamlet's reply is so repressive and scornful that, almost certainly, he has sensed that Ophelia has lied or, at very least, prevaricated. With 'play the fool' he decrees, in fury or sarcasm, that Polonius should father no more daughters like Ophelia. 'Farewell' implies that he starts to leave, only to be held back by Ophelia's prayer. Alternatively, he could be telling her to leave (see, 'Go, farewell,' a few lines later).

134–50   Ophelia says nothing more to Hamlet but holds her ground in face of his verbal onslaught. In many performances, he not only rages against marriage, sexuality and Ophelia herself but alternately throws her aside and violently takes hold of her. The energy of his speeches means that playing the counterfeit madman is an almost impossible alternative at the conclusion of this scene: as Claudius says later, there is 'danger' in what he says and does (ll. 163–8). Ophelia's description of him 'blasted with ecstasy' (l. 161) serves as another stage direction for the actor of Hamlet. Although Claudius says otherwise (see ll. 163–8), the actor and theatre audience may well believe that women, both Ophelia and Gertrude, have 'made [him] mad', without pretence and without being able to prevent it (ll. 143–8).

Threatening death to one who is 'married already' (ll. 148–50) can refer only to Claudius and is often taken as textual evidence that Hamlet knows that he is listening; it is sometimes spoken loudly and pointedly in the direction of the arras behind which the King is concealed. Alternatively, it may imply that Hamlet thinks they are alone, because he would not wish to betray his intention to revenge his father's death. Perhaps it is best played as an instinctive and sudden relaxation of secrecy.

150   As Ophelia remains helpless and silently praying or weeping, Hamlet leaves the stage, continuing to dismiss her with 'To a nunnery go.' The actor may well seek an exceptional way of using these words a fifth time, becoming yet more heartless or more helpless and frustrated. He could speak them through tears or as he positively rushes off stage, wanting to escape and have no more to do with her.

151–62   Ophelia's composure in this soliloquy is more surprising than its contents. Now that she is free from Hamlet's presence and his denunciation and 'ecstasy' (l. 161), her mind functions clearly and consecutively. The return to verse will help the actor to regain control after Ophelia has been emotionally and physically shaken, humiliated, and capable of voicing only conventional prayers. The soliloquy is also important for giving actors and audience an admittedly biased view of Hamlet as he was before his father's murder and his mother's adultery.

163–76   The King's first words will surprise the audience and so may the matter-of-fact way in which he presents his dilemma and plan for action. Once more, the narrative is poised to take a major step forward.

176–81   Having entered his caveat to Claudius's judgement, Polonius turns to his daughter, who has been ignored by both men until this moment. She has probably responded in some non-verbal way to what she is hearing. An audible cry or, perhaps, the beginning of an approach to her father might have prompted him to speak to her.

   The curt dismissal of anything she might be about to say is a cruel humiliation, taking no account of all she has suffered and offering not a word of support. Her silence when addressed will draw the audience's attention to further suffering: she may cry out, shrink visibly, or gather her strength and leave the stage, maintaining her silence. If she is stunned and stands still, she may be left behind at the end of the scene to make her own exit in a different direction from the two men. Once more her love for Hamlet is a strong and still mysterious element of the tragedy: the part the actor has to play is far more demanding and impressive than the words on the page.

181–9   While deferring to the King's judgement, Polonius immediately sets up another occasion for spying on Hamlet, which promises the audience the private encounter with his mother, which, like that with Ophelia, has been long-delayed. Claudius's assent is a reminder of the political consequences of all that Hamlet, as a 'great one', thinks and does.

Act III, scene ii

Starting with prose that is packed with instructions, and Hamlet surrounded with actors getting ready for performance, the action soon gathers pace, with numerous entries and exits, a private meeting of Hamlet and Horatio that sets up another kind of surveillance, and then a royal entry that replicates that of Act I, scene ii, with the addition (in F) of a '*guard carrying torches*'. The audience's attention is then divided between the King and Queen with their Court, Hamlet with Ophelia, and, very soon, the actors in the play that is also a 'trap' (ll. 246–7). After the expected surprise has been sprung, the action proceeds, once more, with short episodes, the first focused on Hamlet and Horatio, the second on Claudius and Hamlet, the last on Gertrude and Hamlet. By these means, the personal dilemmas of the principal persons of the play are more fully revealed than ever before, with Hamlet's mother for the first time present without Claudius and holding centre-stage with her son.

1–54 Judging from the First Player's responses, nothing that Hamlet tells him is unexpected and little needed to be said. His advice to the Players is traditional, with rather more attention to comic performance than in most authorities. Perhaps its chief functions are to provide relief from the tensions and passions of the previous scene and to reveal Hamlet's (rather than Shakespeare's) perfectionist demands on actors – 'O, reform it altogether' (l. 37) – and his wish for performance to 'show virtue her own feature' (l. 22). It also still further shows him to be a well-read, intellectual man, habitually concerned with many possibilities and roused by opposites, both temperance and smoothness, tempest and mere noise (see Commentary at II.ii.432–49).

56–66 Entries and rapid exits quicken the pace and alert the audience; they also serve to mark the difference when Hamlet's call for

Horatio is answered at once, as if he had been waiting for the summons. His 'sweet lord' is a form of address in contrast to all others in this scene – calm, respectful and loyal – soon to be qualified in 'O my dear lord –'.

66–84   Alone, now, with his chosen friend (see ll. 63–5), Hamlet starts by remembering all the 'uses of this world' as he had at the beginning of the play (I.ii.132–7), and recently before meeting Ophelia (III.i.70–7), but now he has no thought of 'self-slaughter'. Although speaking in general terms his words are about physical activity, suffering, and Fortune's 'buffets'. This view of the world leads him to value Horatio as one who 'is not passion's slave'. When he says he will wear such a person in his 'heart of hearts' (ll. 82–4), most Hamlets embrace Horatio; then, with 'Something too much of this,' the moment of intimacy is broken.

85–101   Briefly sharing his plan, Hamlet asks Horatio to help him keep watch on Claudius: if neither of them sees any sign of guilt, either the King is a consummate actor or the Ghost an evil spirit or mere fantasy, bred in Hamlet's subconscious. As he speaks in confidence to the silent Horatio (the speech sounding very like one of the soliloquies), Hamlet knows that all certainties are once more at risk. With Horatio's promise and the trumpets and drums of a royal approach, the two quickly part.

102–18   When asked how he 'fares', Hamlet pretends to be 'idle' (l. 100) and answers with mad-seeming fantasy, his short-phrased speech crammed with imagery and wordplay. Then, without apology, he turns away from the royal presence to address Polonius: although taking charge of proceedings, he is likely to puzzle or confuse everyone. Being so busy contrasts strongly with his retired position and silence when the Court had previously assembled (I.ii). Having made three punishing puns out of one circumstance (ll. 114–15), he allows no time for a reply but turns from Polonius to ask after the Players.

During these exchanges the Court will be forming up as audience for the play around royalty's privileged seats. The presence of the king's bodyguard with '*torches*' (F's stage direction) was, in early daylight performances, a sign of night time and, in any production, will heighten a sense of occasion, and perhaps of ominous consequences.

118–33   Besides longing for intimacy with her son, Gertrude may call for him in an attempt to calm his nerves and his apparent madness. Hamlet's refusal may represent his unfeigned preference, but when he and Ophelia had last parted he was governed by an almost ungovernable repulsion, not an attraction to her (see III.i.121–50). Polonius's remark to the King (l. 120) serves as a reminder of that occasion and their different views of it.

For Ophelia, Hamlet's physical presence will be hard to bear, his physical closeness and string of sexually suggestive jokes heightening her many uncertainties. That she does not find the means to stop him, nor seems to try very hard to find one, may reveal more of her true feelings than anything she says, although 'I think nothing' and 'You are merry' can carry bitter feelings and memories. Both of them speak in short phrases, their words ordinary and yet taunting.

134–44   By the time of his longer and still more outrageous speeches, Hamlet has probably settled on the floor at Ophelia's feet, his head upon her lap, and has gained everyone's attention by a show of apparent madness and an astonishing attack on his mother's infidelity to her dead husband. The actor will have to choose how truly passionate or, even, how truly crazed Hamlet becomes, or whether he is putting on a controlled show of madness.

Either way, Ophelia's feelings as she intervenes with a simple contradiction will be in marked contrast and therefore able to draw the audience's attention to unspoken signs of inward suffering and to Hamlet's intrusive aggression towards her. Again she is a mysterious player in the half-hidden story of their relationship. That both are suffering deeply is likely to be the dominant impression, rather than Hamlet's wilful and unproductive cruelty towards her.

144 (stage direction)   The dumb show and subsequent comments are often omitted in performance, keeping sufficient of the dialogue to introduce the Prologue. Retaining this mimed performance does, however, have the advantage of showing how the interrupted performance of *The Murder of Gonzago* would have concluded. It also frustrates expectation since Claudius betrays no reaction when he sees a representation of a murder that was meant to 'unkennel' (l. 91) his secret guilt: and when the King is silent, Hamlet seems wholly engaged with taunting Ophelia.

One advantage that has been claimed for keeping the dumb show is that, when the text version is played, the audience will be more at liberty to watch the reactions of the King and Queen. Yet the verbal style of what Hamlet will call *The Mousetrap* has highly dramatic qualities that are likely to hold the attention of any audience, even if it knows what will happen. Perhaps Shakespeare did not wish the narrative of the play-within-the-play to be presented too simply. With the two performances in contrasting modes, the comments that follow and accompany them, and the counter-interests of Hamlet's relationship to his mother and Ophelia, and to the actor playing Lucianus, the theatre audience has so much to take its attention that when the King rises 'frighted with false fire' (l. 275) and calls for lights, the happening is as dramatic and unexpected for them as for anyone on stage.

The more attentive spectators may also be puzzled by what happens in the dumb show since the murderer wins the Queen's love after the murder and not before, as previously reported (see I.v.42–57, especially 'adulterate beast' and 'seeming-virtuous'). Shakespeare may have decided at a late date to alter the story of Ambleth and counter all suggestion of Gertrude's adultery before her husband's death (see p. 14, above).

144–57   This duologue between Hamlet and Ophelia can take place while the dumb show is in progress, offering alternative points of focus for the audiences on stage and in the theatre. If the talk follows the show, however, what Hamlet says may be intended to be heard by everyone on stage and so conceal his knowledge of the play and his contribution to the performance. The bawdy jesting with which he finishes may be spoken as part of his pretence of madness and a further concealment of his intentions. The affront to Ophelia might then be an unwilled part of that deception.

158–63   The Prologue gives Hamlet another opportunity to conceal his knowledge of what is about to be performed. 'As woman's love' might be spoken in his mother's direction to the consternation of everyone on stage.

164–238   The text of the play-within-the-play is not easy to read or speak. Strange words and word-order, together with unnecessary amplifications and illustrative metaphors, tend to clog up the formal drive of its rhymed couplets and turn simple statements into generalizing proverbs and riddles. Nevertheless, the most significant speeches conclude with clear statements that strengthen their effect in performance and give climatic, rhythmic and metrical emphasis (see ll. 189–90, 194–5, 221–5, 232–3, and 237–8). In performance, too, the physical enactment of what the text implies makes a strong and easily understood impression.

The result will almost invariably be a slow and stately performance in which references to the sun and moon, day and night, the basic emotions of love, fear, trust and hope, and the conflict of purpose and achievement, join in giving a general as well as a particular 'validity' (l. 199) to the short play. Often the actors wear strange and dignified clothes and their movements are dance-like and accompanied by music. By these means the audience has time to appreciate the re-run of the main story, which includes episodes that were previously only reported. It also will have time to watch the on-stage audience when encouraged to do so by Hamlet's interjections.

190–1   Hamlet's first exclamation is triggered by the presumption that a widow who re-marries has, in some sense, murdered her first husband. This will be the first accusation he makes against his mother in the closet scene (III.iv.29–31) but nowhere does he charge her with murder in a literal sense, nor does the Ghost, or what is subsequently shown in *The Mousetrap*. The idea that re-marriage strikes another mortal blow to a dead husband is bitter like 'wormwood', to both Hamlet and his mother.

In Q2, the very short line 191 is printed in the margin, as if it were not intended to interrupt the Second Player's speech. F and Q1 both read 'Wormwood, Wormwood,' which suggest an impulsive cry rather than a pointed interjection. Either way the comment brings Hamlet back into focus and suggests that the play's effect on his mother, not his uncle, is uppermost in his mind.

196–223 This speech stands out stylistically and requires a more thoughtful and, possibly, a slower delivery. Here *The Mousetrap* reflects more widely on the action of *Hamlet* than elsewhere, not only on Gertrude's love for her first husband but on Hamlet and Claudius as well (see, for example, III.i.84–8 and IV.vii.109–22). When considering Ophelia's role in the play, her steadfastness should, perhaps, be valued in contrast to these other expectations.

234 Although this line is longer and more reflective than line 191, above, Q2 similarly prints this interjection in the margin. Probably, it should also be played as an involuntary comment, indicating Hamlet's close sympathy with his mother; otherwise, it would be a judgemental comment. This is an important decision for the actor.

239–52 The indeterminate quality of 'like' is quickly followed by the deeper implications of 'keep her word', which could mean that the Queen will be faithful to her husband or that she will strike him dead. Hamlet's wordplay at this point could be taken as pretended madness (see 'I must be idle,' l. 100) but, throughout the play, an 'ambiguous giving out' (I.v.178) is a natural feature of his mind, especially when excited by the situation.

With 'poison' (l. 244), Hamlet makes a 'jest' that, if taken literally, would give away the plot of 'The Mousetrap'. The trope or metaphor of that word leads, through 'Tropically', to the ambiguity of 'image', which can mean either a partial or an exact likeness; and so to the ironies of 'knavish' and the comparison of his 'free soul' with that of Claudius and the expectation that he will 'wince'. Here Hamlet's mind is even more volatile and likely to result in a physical performance that contrasts strongly with the deliberately composed appearance of Claudius.

253–63 As at line 145 and in spite of his then becoming 'naught' (l. 156), Ophelia again takes the initiative with Hamlet and, this time,

their talk more quickly becomes sexually provocative. Again Ophelia
will find the encounter painful, since she can neither escape nor
approve, at which point, with a joke about marriage, Hamlet turns
his attention (perhaps mercifully) to the actor of Lucianus. The extent
to which Ophelia suffers and yet takes pleasure in Hamlet's company
is left to the actors to find in rehearsal and performance but the audience is almost certain to become aware of her predicament.

When Lucianus delays speaking – perhaps the actor is prevented
from doing so by Hamlet's outrageous talk – Hamlet orders the play
into violent action. He is likely to be deeply engaged as he delivers a
three-fold order in the idiom of revenge tragedies. 'Begin . . . leave . . .
Come' lead on to an evocation of the 'fatal' harbinger of death,
impatient for its prey (see *Macbeth*, I.iv.37–9).

264–79 Lucianus speaks three couplets in a distinctive verbal style
and rhythm. The single sentence reaches its main verb near the end
of the last line but during this time the audience on stage and in the
theatre can be in no doubt about his intentions. Hamlet has twice
identified him as the 'murderer' (ll. 253 and 261–2) and his 'faces' and
bearing (probably his costume too) will have proclaimed as much
physically. The 'argument' (l. 242) of *The Mousetrap* has taken all this
time to become unambiguously manifest.

As the poison is administered several actions occur almost simultaneously: the Player-King reacts physically to the pain, Hamlet
declares what is happening, Claudius rises to his feet and four people
cry out, each to different purpose. The state occasion is totally
disrupted: Claudius calls for 'light' and leaves the stage, followed by
courtiers, guards, players and everyone except Hamlet and Horatio,
most persons reacting and leaving according to their own unscripted
responses.

All this may happen with the simultaneous effect of a general
mêlée but, if the ordering that is in all the texts is observed, every
other reaction will wait until Hamlet has spoken so that Claudius
'rises' because of his intervention, not because of what the play has
shown. In other words, Hamlet has been caught in his own trap:
besides showing the 'guilt' of Claudius, the play has 'unkennelled' his
own intention to discover the murderer of his father (III.ii.90–1); his

carefully maintained 'cover' has been blown. By showing his knowledge of the play and its double 'argument' of murder and re-marriage, he has revealed the 'something in his soul' that is 'not like madness' (III.i.163–6). His talk of imminent 'revenge' before Lucianus speaks (l. 263) had sent a similar message but only in general terms. The next time Claudius comes on stage he has already taken action to make himself 'safe' (III.iii.1–7) and out of this will grow his plan for 'the present death of Hamlet' (IV.iii.60–70).

Much will depend on how soon Claudius begins to show the effect of what he has been witnessing. Hamlet says it is 'Upon the talk of the poisoning' (l. 298) but that could refer to what has been said by either Lucianus or himself. Perhaps the latter is more likely because Hamlet will immediately speak of himself as a 'player' (ll. 284–9).

280–303   Whatever uncertainties the audience has found in the effect of *The Mousetrap*, Hamlet's elation when alone with Horatio is beyond doubt: it could seem something 'like' madness. For the audience, Horatio's matter-of-fact reactions serve to accentuate the strangeness – possibly, the passion (see ll. 79–84, above) – of Hamlet's behaviour.

At line 300, Hamlet may call for music as the means to calm himself but in many productions he does so because some actors have returned to collect stage properties and, half in jest, he is offering them alternative employment after the sudden end to their acting.

304–32   Hamlet slips back easily into banter with the two 'friends' whom he knows to be spies, starting 'wildly' away from whatever Guildenstern says and claiming that his wit is 'diseased' (ll. 316–17 and 329–30). He has reverted to his 'mad' disguise, as if aware of danger and the need to be secretive.

333–52   As Rosencrantz presses on with his message, Hamlet asks a straight question while continuing an appearance of madness. His reply to a simple aswer is also simple at first – 'We shall obey' (l. 340) – the royal plural signalling a more responsible tone, before relapsing into fake madness. Rosencrantz is sufficiently encouraged by this to speak of their 'love' and friendship (ll. 342 and 346) but Hamlet, joking about betrayal and self-interest, ignores this advance. Their exchange is a travesty of courtly conversation, 'by *these* pickers and stealers' (l. 343) giving opportunity for some physical comedy with the fingers instead of raising the hand for an oath.

The entry for a Player, in a slightly different form in both Q2 and F, may indicate one particular occurrence among what the actors have been doing to clear their properties from the stage. Alternatively, it may be a delayed answer to Hamlet's call at lines 300–3.

353–79   Turning to Guildenstern, who has often proved the more intelligent and persistent of the two (see III.i.7 and Commentary), Hamlet vents his anger at this friend's betrayal in a controlled and cumulative way that mixes satire with irony. In performance, on 'these ventages' (l. 365), he will often place the instrument in Guildenstern's hands, so bringing the two young men close together, to his 'friend's' very evident embarrassment.

380–94   Keyed up with excitement and anger, Hamlet turns on Polonius before he can speak and then answers his urgent message by mocking the experienced counsellor's ability to make distinctions and change his opinion. The curt 'I will say so' (l. 393) carries an implied rebuke for Hamlet's fooling, made all the sharper in that Hamlet has just said that it is he who is being fooled, not Polonius. The separate *Exit* for Polonius is taken from F, after which the request to his 'friends' and their departure probably come as a surprise.

Horatio has said nothing since line 299 when he was closely sharing in Hamlet's dilemma, advising and encouraging him. In the first Act also, after Hamlet had seen the Ghost, Horatio had dropped out of the action as if his lack of 'passion' meant that he did not function easily in Hamlet's world. Later, he will fail to keep 'good watch' over Ophelia (IV.v.74).

395–406   After the varied encounters that followed the break-up of the actors' performance, the focus settles once more on Hamlet, alone on stage. When he speaks it is to mark the hellishness of what is about to happen, much as Lucianus had done (see ll. 264–9): he imagines himself drinking the 'hot blood' of recent wounds and transgressing the bonds that maintain peace in the world. He is no longer the 'gentle' young prince and has to hold back from an instinct to kill his mother (as Nero had done). What he might do is so frightening to him that he leaves the stage, barely under control.

This soliloquy, coming near the centre of the tragedy, shorter and more transforming than most others, is a major landmark in Hamlet's 'journey' through the play and a defining moment for each performance of the role. His instinctive cruelty towards his mother can be his most deep-seated feeling, which needs to be allayed (in III.iv) before he can avenge his father's death. On the other hand, this exceptional talk in the vein of a revenge play may be the result of a feigned or real madness and the clear oppositions of the soliloquy's concluding lines the hard-won success of a rational mind that has to struggle with a nightmarish imagination.

Act III, scene iii

Attention passes to Claudius for the first time since the break-up of the Court. After despatching immediate business, he is alone in his private apartment and, although he does not know this, he is soon in the presence of the newly dangerous Hamlet. There is so much that is inconclusive in this scene, or remains in process, that it does little to advance the play's narrative. Its main effects are to report plans for sending Hamlet to England, offer new insights into Claudius's mind, and show Hamlet unwilling to take revenge in an unplanned and private situation.

1–26 Charged with accompanying Hamlet to England, both fellow students speak only of their duty to the King and are ready with the traditional arguments in favour of a monarch's prerogative and responsibility to his subjects. These political ideas had recently brought years of peace to England and, for early audiences, would have drawn the play's Denmark closer to their own country as Elizabeth's reign drew to a close. Guildenstern is the more cunning in expressing subservience but both speak as if they had plenty of time for flattery and expressing their conformity; they appear very differently from when they were skirmishing with Hamlet.

Although in danger and responsible for the 'cess' of his brother's 'majesty' (ll. 15–16), Claudius maintains his usual political decisiveness. However, when his opening words urge speed, he may betray an underlying 'fear' (l. 25) that is not verbally acknowledged until he despatches his nephew's two 'minders'.

27–35 As if he has been waiting for Rosencrantz and Guildenstern to leave, Polonius enters unannounced, using his privileged right of access. Short-phrased sentences suggest haste but he delays his departure to justify what he has contrived and, by the way, flatter the King. The pace of the action has quickened.

36 In half a line, Claudius acknowledges the hidden guilt that previously has been openly expressed only in the brief soliloquy as Ophelia is about to become a trap to catch Hamlet's secret thoughts (III.i.49–54). But an audience may have caught traces of it underneath his spoken words, in signs of haste, avoidance, or uncertainty, as in the dialogue earlier in this scene.

36–72 Claudius expresses his guilt in physical images ('rank . . . smells . . . sharp . . . defeats . . . bound'), with displaced word-order and sentences that follow each other abruptly, as if thoughts have a pressured force. A contrary impulse intervenes when the thought of his hand thick with blood leads on to 'the sweet heavens' (l. 45), mercy, and the 'twofold force' of prayer. With 'I'll look up' (l. 50), he imagines that his fault is past, but former pressures are still at work under the short hopeful utterance and he finds he cannot pray. Imagining himself a prisoner before a judge, he knows that only repentance would be of use and his argument gives way to cries of horror and helplessness. Now words express a very palpable struggle in which 'angels' and a 'new-born babe' are opposed to a 'bosom black as death' (ll. 67–71).

'*He kneels*' comes from Q1, which contains other stage directions that read like eye-witness reports of performance. Such an action, with eyes closed in prayer, makes Hamlet's unseen entrance plausible and provides him with a reason for not killing the King immediately (see ll. 84–8, below). After the verbal and emotional struggles of the soliloquy (and as lines 70–1 indicate), the act of kneeling will be slow and painful.

'All may be well' (l. 72) gives the audience no clear notion of what the kneeling implies. But the soliloquy has just established beyond all doubt that this revenge tragedy takes place in a society fully aware of Christian thought and practice. Some recent productions have taken the hint and located this scene in a private chapel and placed a crucifix upon its altar.

73–96   Because Hamlet speaks for himself, this speech can be considered as one in the sequence of soliloquies but it stands apart from the others because his mind is focused on Claudius and the present moment. Usually the actor speaks from behind Claudius's back so that it is plausible that his victim cannot hear and that Hamlet could, in the instant, kill him. At line 74 in Q1, Hamlet says 'Ay so, come forth and work thy last', implying that here he draws his sword.

The word 'pat' and the repetition of 'now' suggest that Hamlet starts without any deep thought. The short phrases that follow represent a quick-thinking mind that holds back from speech on the incomplete line 78. Considering the consequences that would follow the killing, Hamlet recovers a more usual form of speech, conscious of implications, responsive to physical actuality, and expressive of feeling in metaphor and epithet. A question once formulated is unambiguously answered and, after a pause at line 87, acted upon.

The decision having been made to postpone revenge for a more punishing occasion, all tension relaxes and Hamlet's imagination feeds greedily on other satisfying and terrible possibilities. He finds more 'relish' here than elsewhere in answering the call to revenge and sending Claudius to hell, perhaps because no action is needed at this moment. He leaves to go to his mother without hesitation.

97 to the end   These words are easily understood, even as they declare that words are not the same as thoughts. In performance, however, an ambiguity remains in *how* Claudius stops praying. Does he rise to his feet willingly, reluctantly, purposefully, or unsteadily? Does he speak before, during, or after rising? Is he going to bed or does he intend to watch through the night? From now on, the audience will hear more about Claudius's thoughts, but what they are at this moment depends very much on the actor: how much weariness, despair, renewed determination, or desire for peace and forgiveness is evident in these words and in his subsequent exit from the stage.

Act III, scene iv

In present-day productions, a large bed is usually placed centre-stage for this scene although a 'closet' (III.ii.338–9 and III.iii.27) was a private chamber, not a bedroom. This later stage practice is well established because it encourages the close physical intimacy that the text requires and emphasizes the thematic and narrative importance of this first and only private meeting of the tragic hero and his mother. Played without a bed, the action may become more violent and outrageous as the two actors struggle with each other on the stage floor or overturn whatever furniture has been provided.

1–9 Hamlet's words from off stage are not in Q2 but come from F and Q1. However, in all three texts he is heard as he approaches, as if he is hurrying or rapidly opening closed doors; his first abrupt words to his mother carry on that impulsive impression.

10–18 The echoing, one-line speeches suggest a deliberate stand-off, neither person welcoming or giving way to the other, or disclosing more than is judged necessary; a tension between them can be very obvious as meanings twist and change. The dance-like pattern is broken with Hamlet's answer to the Queen's second question, after which, with her line 18, she probably stands or moves further apart from him.

19–23 Hamlet's commanding tone, which has grown over the last few lines, and the brusque use of 'budge' and 'go not', suggest a strength of purpose and even violence, as he insists on a close encounter. In performance he may catch hold of his mother roughly and this makes her cry out for help, thinking he is about to murder her. But his very look and tone of voice may be sufficiently frightening to motivate this reaction.

With Polonius's cry from behind the arras, action, exclamations and accusations all escalate. As line 33 will make clear, Hamlet thinks he is killing the King, but the body may lie behind the arras so that he cannot be sure whom he has struck until he sees and addresses the dead body at line 32.

Even if Hamlet discovers Polonius immediately after 'Is it the King?' rather than later, his own 'bloody deed' can so disturb his mind that he almost blurts out the secret of his father's murder. Or, possibly, he is so keyed up that the retort to his mother is spoken coldly – even, slowly – with a bitter, deadly precision.

As Gertrude repeats his 'As kill a king' she may think that he is accusing her of murdering his father, for so line 30 could imply, rather than being an allusion to the consequences of her second marriage (see III.ii.188–95 and Commentary). Any misunderstanding will not be lifted by Hamlet's reply, which ensures a continuing awkwardness and uncertainty between them.

32–4 Hamlet's epitaph for Polonius, spoken immediately after killing him, is comprehensive in its dismissal of any prudence or love the old counsellor and father has shown (compare II.ii.153–6 and 401–7). At this moment, Hamlet is either 'rash' himself or totally determined, his immediate need to confront his mother intruding on all other concerns. Nevertheless, this first death on stage will have a direct effect on the audience and it is likely that Hamlet's disregard of it will also register strongly.

35–54 Gertrude's two interjections provide instruction for the actor of Hamlet to speak loudly and violently but he starts by recognizing her unspoken grief and then, ironically, calling for 'Peace' – the stillness and silence for which he yearns repeatedly (see I.ii.129–30; III.i.60–4; V.ii.352, etc.). Once more insisting that she sits down (see l. 19, above), he may sit beside her before his words become aggressive (drawing on military metaphors) and so 'rude' that he 'roars' and 'thunders' – or so his mother says. Yet his thoughts are also at war

within himself, as he speaks of 'grace . . . modesty . . . innocent love
. . . [and] sweet religion' alongside 'a blister . . . dicers' oaths . . . A
rhapsody of words . . . [and] the Doom' of the entire world.

53–68   In reaction to his mother's protests and incomprehension,
Hamlet turns away to a 'picture' of his father, and then to one of his
uncle. How he does this in performance has changed over the
centuries. At one time, he pointed to portraits on the wall of the
'closet', and later, to miniatures hanging around his and Gertrude's
necks, or to two coins that he draws from his pocket. In modern-
dress productions, photographs have been used, either carried in a
wallet or pocket book or found in a newspaper or journal.

   However the business is managed, the change of focus alters how
he speaks. He is now both reasonable and enthusiastic as he
constructs a glowing and mythical image of his father before
dismissing his mother's new husband as diseased and barren.
Having both portraits in his gaze, perhaps in his hands, brings more
measured and ordered speech until he turns away from them to
address his mother.

69–89   Denying that she could 'love' a new husband at her 'age' – if
he is 30 years old, she must be in her mid-forties or older – Hamlet
attacks his mother's sanity. After the incomplete line 82 suggests a
major pause, he attacks her with harsh satire as a shameless 'matron',
unable to see reason.

89–103   By some point – varying with each change of cast and,
probably, with each performance – Gertrude has listened and her
mind has changed. This does not stop his out-pouring of words so
that she unavailingly cries out 'no more' three times and, even then,
it is the Ghost's entry that eventually silences him.

   As Hamlet will change in voice and bearing when his denunciation of the 'rank sweat' and 'stewed' corruption of the marriage bed
leads on to the charge of murder and its political consequences, so
signs of guilt, suffering and horror will become more evident in
Gertrude. His 'words' wound 'like daggers' and yet, once more, he is
'sweet Hamlet' (ll. 95–7): her 'soul' is in turmoil, as both she and the

Ghost describe what is happening (see ll. 90–2 and 114). At last, 'No more' is all she says, both reproof and confession silenced.

Both actors have to present persons driven by strong passion and with their reason threatened; both are also bound together as mother and fatherless son. The demands of this encounter are extreme and no other scene in the play can adequately prepare the actors for meeting them. Many variations are possible in performance. Have they moved apart and does either one of them try to maintain physical contact? Is Gertrude trying to calm Hamlet, rather than answer his accusations? How strong and how much in evidence is their love for each other? By the end, is Hamlet expressing hatred for Claudius, rather than trying to remonstrate with his mother? However played, the scene engages them both at a deep level of consciousness and their relationship is bound to be different afterwards.

104–40 Incomplete verse-lines (variously set out by editors) indicate a pause or disruption in Hamlet's speech before, in two full verse-lines, he prays for heavenly protection and then addresses the Ghost. If he has knelt for the prayer, he could remain kneeling for the submissive words that follow.

Gertrude's 'he's mad' establishes at once that she cannot see the Ghost and, therefore, that this apparition is different, at least in purpose, from the one that had been visible to everyone on the battlements in Act I. It also underlines what is implied in his speech, that mother and son have suddenly and completely lost contact with each other. She immediately believes he is hallucinating, as she tells him later: see, especially, 'This is the very coinage of your brain . . .' (ll. 138–40). In this she may well be right, although the audience will at first believe it is the same Ghost as before (it will, doubtless, be the same actor). This time the apparition could well be the product of his 'fantasy' (I.i.23) and not a spirit of any kind: it is in no obvious pain but is 'gracious . . . pale . . . piteous', and it 'glares'. A stage direction in Q1 says that it is '*in his nightgown*', not the complete armour of a Danish military hero (see I.i.60–1). Moreover, it tells Hamlet nothing he did not previously know.

After Hamlet has spoken to his mother and she only echoes his question (ll. 116–17), he falls silent but continues to look at the Ghost, his eyes and presence both alarmed and wild. She remains entirely concerned with Hamlet, whom, despite his reactions, she now addresses as her 'gentle son' (l. 123). The two remain at odds until the now-silent Ghost has gone, when the word 'ecstasy' [*mad, incapable in mind*] shows Hamlet what he has to prove in order to be understood.

141–57   He has probably taken her hand in his to repudiate the charge. He is careful and earnest, his speech now as 'temperate' as his pulse. Having reassured her about his sanity, he uses overtly religious terms ('for love of grace . . . Confess yourself to heaven', ll. 145 and 150) to urge her to 'repent', as any good Christian would believe necessary and effective. (There are echoes here from the previous scene when Claudius attempted to repent.) More unexpectedly, Hamlet acknowledges his own need to be forgiven, and here, too, is a Christian theme found in every repetition of the Lord's Prayer: 'Forgive us our trespasses as we forgive them that trespass against us.'

Everything has changed between mother and son: closer together in mind than ever before and speaking thoughts only hinted at previously, probably they are physically close as well. Gertrude no longer protests: her one-line response acknowledges that he has shattered her heart; how slowly, calmly, quietly, lovingly, or in how much pain she speaks will depend on the performances of both actors. Beyond doubt is the delicacy of the situation, in which the audience senses the turning of a tide of feeling: the drama stands still at a point of mutual dependence.

158–60   Hamlet's 'O' echoes his mother's at the beginning of the previous line but she spoke of the present moment, he speaks of the future. With 'Good night' (l. 160), a familiar and intimate phrase, he returns to the present and confirms their new closeness. Four more times in this scene he will say 'good night', which the actor is able to vary each time so that they mark a growing awareness of their relationship and interdependence.

160–71   As Hamlet had pretended to madness so, now, he recommends a pretence of virtue as a way for his mother to escape from sexual dependence on his uncle. He has become more understanding (perhaps sympathetic) and the change will be evident in his voice and manner. Instead of confrontation, they may sit side by side, making physical contact with their hands or looking attentively at each other.

171–80   'Once more' suggests that Hamlet is about to leave. His thoughts have again moved to the future and, from that, to the mutual forgiveness and respect that should replace antagonism. But that prospect brings him back to the man he has killed; perhaps as he turned to go, he saw his corpse on the floor of the stage. A ready repentance is almost at once modified by a sense of inevitability. The idea that 'heaven' played a part in what has happened is one that will recur later; see 'even in that was heaven ordinant' and 'If it be not now, yet it will come' (V.ii.48 and 213–17).

Prefixing his words by 'So again', as if aware of the difficulty of leaving, he wishes his mother 'good night' and is about to leave yet another time. In the kind of generalizing couplet that usually marks an immediate exit, he then looks back on his 'cruel' acts and 'kind' intentions, as if thinking of the world he had been born 'to right' – to use the words of an earlier, strongly placed couplet (I.v.188–9). And still he cannot leave his mother without 'one word more' and so he stops, and before he can say anything, Gertrude asks what she should do. They are thinking together, now.

182–200   In reply to her simple question, Hamlet starts by repeating the advice already given but with a new repugnance towards the love-making of his mother and her new husband, which he describes in more intimate and graphic detail. This leads to a crucial instruction that will protect the disguise of madness he wishes to maintain (see ll. 188–9). He continues to express these two concerns, about himself and about her. After the incomplete verse-line 197, Gertrude intervenes with a solemn promise, after which another incomplete line suggests a shared silence, during which they may well embrace. Mutual trust has been established; when he next speaks, Hamlet changes the subject, turning again to the future.

201–18   After the strong passions and wrenching nerves of their long encounter, Hamlet speaks in a new, matter-of-fact way about what will happen next. She responds just as simply but with regret. Both know they are going with the tide of events (see 'must' and 'concluded') but then thoughts of his treacherous 'schoolfellows' turn Hamlet's thoughts to what he is able to do: his mind quickens, with metaphor, wordplay, irony, jest, decisiveness, very much in an earlier manner.

To cover his tracks Hamlet knows he must remove Polonius's body and, in saying so, his joking becomes brutal and dismissive where only moments before he had been respectful and sober (compare ll. 213 and 214–17 with 173–8). Here he may be so unfeeling that he seems to revert to a form of madness or crazed insensitivity. As if trying to retain his sanity and new-found tenderness, he twice repeats 'good night' in two different, almost imperative, forms, so that 'mother' is his last word as he leaves her speechless. And all this time, he must struggle with the dead weight of the man he has killed and who is the father of Ophelia, to whom he had declared his love.

Although the long-delayed meeting of mother and son has exposed and resolved much that was previously hidden, it will leave a theatre audience wanting to know more: he is now a murderer; she, having been silent for most of the last sixty lines, has taken on the new responsibility of protecting her son's secrecy. The political revenge tragedy about a *'Prince of Denmark'* has also become an intimate and passionate play about a mother and her son.

Performed at or near the midpoint of this tragedy on a large and familiar stage in ordinary daylight for more than a thousand spectators, this sustained and innovative scene was an amazing achievement. And to this day, in very different theatrical and cultural contexts, it can still ground the play's action in instinctive and imaginative responses. For some spectators, the actors' presence and heartbeats – as well as narrative, words, and physical actions – have become eloquent and hold rapt attention.

ACT IV

In comparison with earlier, Hamlet has little to say or do in the seven scenes of this Act. Now Claudius, Laertes, and Ophelia come into prominence, and Fortinbras is seen for the first time. In the absence of any large-scale scene with many persons on stage, dramatic focus changes frequently and attention is held by a series of crises. As the narrative continues to develop strongly, both on and off stage, an audience will increasingly sense that the tragedy is drawing much closer to its conclusion and that all depends on the return of Hamlet to Elsinore to face the consequences of his actions.

Act IV, scene i

Most editors assume that Gertrude remains in view of the audience between the Acts. This contravenes the usual Shakespearean practice of clearing the stage between scenes, and ignores an entry for her in Q2 at the start of the new scene (reproduced in the Penguin edition), but neither stage direction nor dialogue in any of the early texts indicates that Gertrude leaves the stage at the end of Act III. With the business of that Act concluded, a new movement of the narrative starts with the entry of Claudius and his discovery of his wife in obvious distress.

Late at night (see l. 29), the short scene starts with a question and will soon mark a change in the relationship between Gertrude and Claudius as the dialogue becomes fraught, with her very noticeable silence after line 28, and concludes with his admission of a troubled 'soul'.

1–12 Rosencrantz and Guildenstern presumably enter because Claudius has called for them, but they leave almost at once on Gertrude's insistence, having said or done nothing to any purpose. The incomplete lines 3 and 6 indicate pauses before Gertrude, with a troubled and bewildered metaphor, reports that Hamlet is hopelessly mad and uses this to excuse his killing of Polonius. Sighs and tears have given place to careful speech as she does Hamlet's bidding.

12–28 At once Claudius is alert to his own danger and then to wider 'threats'. His mind moves quickly: questioning what his response should be, seeing blame attaching to himself, finding an excuse in his 'love' for Hamlet, which has acted like a disease. He probably remains standing and moving about restlessly, while

Gertrude sits and says what more she can, probably weeping as she speaks of Hamlet's tears. She then becomes entirely silent for the rest of the scene.

29 to the end Following a wordless 'O', Claudius calls Gertrude to 'come away', but neither of them leaves the stage: his 'majesty and skill' (l. 31) is on trial; he has business to do without delay and before dawn. When he calls Guildenstern, both he and Rosencrantz reappear immediately, as if they had been waiting outside the door.

As they 'haste' off (l. 37) to get help with seeking out Hamlet and disposing of the body, Claudius speaks partly to Gertrude and partly to himself – the proportion is variable – and sounding less decisive than before and more unsure of what will be the outcome. Another inarticulate 'O' precedes the end of the scene. He may leave before she does, as if more absorbed in his own problems than concerned for her. Or she may leave at once so that his concluding line is a brief soliloquy of self-awareness or, possibly, of determination to counter his growing fears.

Act IV, scene ii

This unusually short scene starts with a chase and may finish with one. The overall tempo is rapid and, if the '*attendants*' ('*others*', Q2) are numerous and carry drawn swords (see IV.iii.14), action can be visually impressive: danger is in the air, especially when Hamlet reverts to aggressive and 'mad' behaviour.

1–22 Hamlet having just disposed of the body of the old man he has killed, any relief that may be expressed in 'Safely stowed' is quickly dispelled and turns to harsh humour as Rosencrantz questions him. Their exchange is taut and on Hamlet's part evasive, mocking, and then, as verse turns to prose, threatening. All signs of friendship are gone.

23 to the end When Hamlet lightly brushes aside what has been said, Rosencrantz tells him what he 'must' do and this triggers a paradoxical and puzzling response. He could mean that both King and body are in the palace but not together (perhaps with the implication that the King may soon be dead, as Polonius is). Or he might imply that the body is dead like that of the true king (his father). Or, taking a wider view and speaking as 'the son of a king' (l. 13), he may be distinguishing the King's physical body from that of his office and be about to continue on this theme. As the verbal exchange ends or trails away ambiguously, Guildenstern takes over from his fellow, as he has done on other occasions when the going got rough (see Commentary at III.i.1–28).

Hamlet answers with wordplay on thing/*no*thing and then submits to be being brought to the King under guard, as he will appear in the following scene. Such playfulness in the circumstances leaves everyone speechless.

'Hide fox, and all after' (found only in F) comes from a child's game of hide and seek and implies that, as the guard readies itself to move off in one direction, Hamlet suddenly leaves in another, surprising them all and laughing at them. Some editors omit this, as one of numerous additions that actors may have made to Shakespeare's text. In performance, however, it gives a welcome spurt of new energy at the end of a scene in which the action has developed little: it shows Hamlet fooling others 'to the top of [his] bent' (III.ii.391) as he prepares to encounter Claudius.

Act IV, scene iii

This more formal scene (possibly a council meeting, like II.ii and III.i) starts with Claudius attended with his 'wisest friends' (IV.i.38), who are soon joined by '*all the rest*' (Q2). Everyone knows that Polonius has been killed and so a general tension is felt on stage that becomes more focused with Hamlet's appearance under guard. A stand-off is established when Claudius tries to take control and Hamlet, pretending madness, aggressively mocks death, kings, commoners, heaven, hell and, finally, marriage.

The scene closes with its focus narrowed on Claudius, who reveals in soliloquy that he will use the political power of Denmark to ensure Hamlet's death. ('*Exeunt all but the King*' is another stage direction taken from Q1.) The scene unsettles an audience's expectations:

initiative has been taken away from the hero of the tragedy, who is travelling off stage, attended by the King's accomplices and about to enter a trap.

1–11 Preparing his counsellors for pre-emptive action, Claudius acknowledges the popular attraction of Hamlet and his own 'desperate' condition. Although a public statement, his speech has the self-aware deliberation of a soliloquy, linking it to the concluding couplet of his previous scene (IV.i.40–5). If line 7 is spoken as two incomplete verse-lines with a silence between them, the 'eyes' of an audience may recognize the outward and physical signs of Claudius's inner guilt.

11–38 After rapid coming and going, question and answer, Hamlet is brought on stage under guard and is immediately interrogated without deference to his rank (compare 'Our chiefest courtier cousin, and our son', I.ii.117). His first answer, provocatively brief and unexpected, gives Claudius little option but to ask again (probably humouring the supposed madman). That gives Hamlet the cue for an elaborate verbal joke as he takes his time, with prose once again superseding verse. The implicit challenge to the superiority of a 'king' over a 'beggar' leaves Claudius no option but to ask again and so feed Hamlet's clownish fooling.

At lines 32–3, when Hamlet at last answers the King's 'Where is Polonius?' with an invitation to go to hell ('th'other place'), audiences are likely to laugh with the 'mad' and 'dangerous' prisoner (l. 2 above). Even jokes about the decomposing corpse of the murdered counsellor are likely to be greeted with laughter. There is sufficient 'method' in the madness (II.ii.205–6) for an audience to know that it is not real and to suspect that Claudius thinks so too.

39–55 Returning to verse, Claudius's sustained speech brings the exchange back to a formal interrogation, with himself as king and judge dealing with a subject and prisoner. Hamlet hears nothing new (see III.iv.203–4) and continues to play the fool and mock Claudius's pronouncements. With a parting attack on the King's marriage (which Claudius tries to take seriously), he promptly leaves the stage.

'Come, for England' is usually spoken as a taunting flourish as

Hamlet goes before he is ordered to do so. Alternatively it can provide a moment of serious thought as he remembers the dangers he had acknowledged earlier (see III.iv.203–11).

Hamlet's pretended madness is so aggressively directed towards Claudius and, in the end, so nearly reveals his secret 'purposes' (l. 49), that the pretence seems to give him pleasure or, possibly, to show that he is touched with a real craziness. Since 'Farewell, dear mother' is a near echo of the repeated 'Good night, mother' of the closet scene, Hamlet may be mocking Claudius by replicating the physical closeness of the conclusion of that scene. On these words in some recent productions, Hamlet has forced a kiss on Claudius's lips.

56 to the end   Claudius takes charge, urging 'speed' and 'haste'. Soon he is alone once more and, as he addresses the absent King of England, a complex sentence unfurls steadily over the course of eight lines, ending with his unambiguous intention to bring about Hamlet's death. 'Do it, England' quickens and strengthens the pulse of his words and is followed by a naked, unflinching statement of what is at risk – for himself, rather than for the Danish state. These feelings have been implied at the start of the scene but now they are stated unequivocally: then the actor has to turn away and walk off stage, his back to many in the audience whose understanding and expectations have just been heightened.

Act IV, scene iv

For the first time, the action moves away from Elsinore as sounds of a marching army are heard and non-Danish uniforms are seen on stage.

The Folio text prints little more than Fortinbras's first speech: Hamlet and his attendants do not enter and the Captain does not remain to explain what is happening. Such an unheralded and largely unexplained entry for a person who will have a significant impact on the conclusion of the play is without parallel in Shakespeare's plays but the recent Oxford editors were so sure that F represents Shakespeare's own revision of Q2 that they accepted its version without further question (see pp. 7–8, above).

Following the text of Q2 (as the great majority of editors have done) brings Hamlet back to the audience, no longer feigning madness but establishing his own grasp of what has happened and what he must now do. By marking the contrast provided by Fortinbras, he considers his own destiny and what is needed to be called 'great'. He concludes by reaffirming, more harshly, his determination to avenge his father's death. This soliloquy gives a far stronger focus on Hamlet, before an absence of some 440 lines, than the 'mad' exit from the previous scene, and it leaves an audience waiting for the outcome. It also more strongly establishes Fortinbras in the audience's mind before his entry in the final scene.

1–8 The brief appearance of Fortinbras is made visually and aurally impressive by his marching army, probably with drum accompaniment. Because they are in transit, not on parade, no banners are carried from which Hamlet could know their allegiance. Fortinbras's concluding order implies that the soldiers are halted before he speaks: this means that his words will be clearly heard and all further action will wait upon them.

9–31 This duologue is unhurried, both speakers taking time to reflect on the military and moral issues involved. Presumably soldiers are heard for some time from off stage as they march off on their mission. The meeting leaves Hamlet thoughtful so that Rosencrantz, not heeding his frame of mind, is quickly sent on ahead, the others leaving with him.

32–66 The experienced First Player had previously prompted Hamlet to blame himself for inaction (see II.ii.547–603) and now the young soldier Fortinbras produces the same response together with two new questions: Why should any man delay, and what is the nature of greatness (see ll. 53–6)?

The concluding couplet lacks the practicality and precision of II.ii.602–3 but, unlike that earlier resolve, it is spoken while considering the possibility of failure. Hamlet has not previously been so thoughtfully determined to shed blood. His exit may well be swift, leaving the audience in doubt as to what he will do next.

Act IV, scene v

Throughout this scene, the longest and most varied in the Act, dramatic focus centres on Ophelia except for the totally unexpected turn of events that brings Laertes back from Paris to revenge his father, accompanied by a crowd – a 'riotous head' – crying out that he should be king (see ll. 101–10). As Claudius tries to placate him, Ophelia re-enters and Laertes has to fight back tears as, ineffectually, he tries to make contact with her. Swiftly Claudius takes charge and draws the scene to a close that leaves much unresolved.

1–10 Both Horatio and '*a Gentleman*' enter with the Queen in Q2 but in F only Horatio is present: he speaks the Gentleman's lines and Gertrude the two that Q2 gives to Horatio (ll. 14–15), only then revealing her own fears. If both men have applied pressure on the Queen (as in Q2), the guilt and fear expressed in lines 7 to 10 will have an added prominence as her first personal utterance since the opening scene of the Act.

In the Folio version, Horatio returns to the stage after a long absence and immediately leaves to let Ophelia enter. In the text of Q2, he can remain throughout the scene as a passive witness to events, until Claudius orders him to follow Ophelia off stage (l. 94). In both versions, the focus is on Gertrude's suffering immediately before Ophelia re-enters the play, truly mad in contrast to Hamlet's pretended madness. This is one of several occasions when Shakespeare drew the audience's attention to these two together, the two women in Hamlet's life, who have been given little to say in comparison with other major roles; their presence is often more significant than what they say (see III.i.38–42 and 111–50; III.ii.118–19; and V.i.239–42).

11–40 Lines 4–13 have prepared the audience to be puzzled by what Ophelia says and does. If her first words are spoken to Gertrude, not recognizing who she is, they will be an instance of this. Her first song is also puzzling in that it could refer either to Gertrude or to herself, before veering off to the life of a holy pilgrim. The next stanza might relate either to her father or to a 'true-love' who is imagined as dead (ll. 13 and 40). But certain elements in what she says and does are abundantly clear: the isolation that her distraction brings, even when making contact with Gertrude; her determination to speak and sing; her idealism and strength of feeling; and the unsophisticated rural world of her imagination.

Ophelia's 'mad scenes' would have been a formidable challenge for a boy actor in early performances and they are so today for young actresses, especially when speech and singing are accompanied by the violent, repetitive actions reported in lines 5–6 and 11. In the early version of the play represented by Q1, she had entered '*playing on a lute, and her hair down, singing*' but in that text her part consists of little except the songs. The sudden and unexpected transitions of Q2 and F were probably later additions since they could scarcely be managed while playing, or carrying, a lute.

41–67 The King intervenes to rather less effect than the Queen. Both become speechless and must stand around, unable to help, while Ophelia makes little consecutive sense but interacts with others and twice blesses them (see ll. 42 and 44).

Her second song (ll. 48–66) is not about an ideal love or death, as her first had been, but about disappointment in love and loss of virginity. Some actors and critics have taken this to represent the facts of Ophelia's relationship with Hamlet. But more consistent with the tenor of dialogue elsewhere in the play is the view that Ophelia has imagined herself into this situation through fear of rejection or in response to Hamlet's repeated talk of sexual mismatches and brutality (see III.i.111–50; and III.ii.153–5 and 255–62).

This second song starts in the present tense, establishes a dramatic immediacy, and concludes with reported speech, all of which will invite the singer to enact the events as the story develops. In performance the song tends to draw the theatre audience to share in Ophelia's predicament.

67–74 Claudius having turned away to speak to Gertrude, Ophelia speaks again of the future ('we know . . . not what we may be', l. 44) until she begins to act as if she were a grand lady and, unexpectedly, takes herself off stage. The King reacts at once, having heard for himself what 'Dangerous conjectures' she could spread around the Court (ll. 14–15).

75–97 After the exceptional and affecting intervention of Ophelia's madness, Claudius's long speech serves for the audience the useful, and possibly necessary, purpose of re-establishing the narrative facts and their implications. And it adds the significant news that Laertes has returned in secret and is spreading the belief that Claudius, the King, has had his father murdered.

In his more usual and masterly way, Claudius mixes report with self-appraisal and general reflections but now he also speaks openly to Gertrude of his own suffering (ll. 95–7). His appeals to his wife here and at the start of the speech remain unanswered, as had his three calls for her to 'come away' at the end of their previous scene together (IV.i). As if filling a vacuum, the audience's attention will be drawn to silences and whatever physical signs of unspoken thoughts are evident. Does she respond when he speaks her name or refers to her son's violence? Does he move closer to her at any point? Is 'O my dear Gertrude' (l. 95) a response to signs of her alarm or is it motivated only by his own need for reassurance and fellowship?

98–112 Sounds of insurrection are heard just as Claudius on several counts imagines his own death. Elsinore has been stormed and the Switzers [*mercenary soldiers*] of the royal guard have been overcome or eluded. A single messenger gives graphic details and the stage direction for '*noise within*' (in Q2 and F) indicates that he speaks against a continuing sound of riot and outcry. A *coup d'état* is imminent and, in performance, much will depend on the off-stage sounds: how threatening and numerous the insurgents seem to be, how violently they break open the doors.

When Gertrude cries out that Laertes is not on the right track to find his father's murderer (ll. 111–12), she presumably believes Hamlet to be safely in England and is instinctively playing for time.

113–22 Claudius is defenceless without his 'Switzers' (l. 99) but then, amazingly, Laertes sends his followers – those who would make him king (ll. 108–10) – to a safe distance. Above everything else he wants to be given his father's body and know the truth about his death (see ll. 130 and 132) but, once alone with Claudius, his hatred and suspicions surface in 'O thou vile King' (l. 117).

In many performances, Laertes holds his sword's point at the King's throat so that only Gertrude can urge him to be calm and appeal to his goodness. However this is played, his next words make very clear that he is ready to shed blood. In a society with no recourse to justice higher than the king, his words would be more chilling for staking the honour of his father and mother, as well as his own, in active pursuit of revenge.

122–55 'Let him go, Gertrude', which is found in all three early texts, indicates that she has grasped hold of Laertes while he is face-to-face with Claudius. This makes difficulties for actors when Gertrude is played as a weak-minded person but the order is repeated at line 128 so that there can be no doubt that she makes some physical attempt to restrain the armed and impassioned young man. whose rebellion looks 'so giant-like' (l. 123). Moments later she intervenes verbally (l. 130) and is again dissuaded.

When Claudius does respond (perhaps after Laertes has turned to reply to Gertrude), his words are remarkably calm and open minded, although for the audience it is highly ironic that the murderer and traitor claims that he is invincible by virtue of the divine right of kings. (See, for example, *Richard II*, III.ii.43–58.) Some spectators may realize that he is being devious because he knows very well who killed Polonius and, unlike Gertrude, is not troubled by any threat to Hamlet. He is carefully 'talking down' Laertes' rage and by line 150 knows that any threat to himself is over.

Laertes is silent until Claudius orders, 'Speak, man' (l. 129), and again after he has been briefly and inconclusively answered. But in performance the audience will surely see that he is in no way passive during his silences because, when he does speak, his demands are backed by disavowing 'allegiance . . . conscience and grace' in favour of damnation in order to be 'Most throughly' revenged. The contrast to Hamlet's doubts and delays could scarcely be greater.

Carefully, Laertes is made to realize he need not be alone in seeking revenge and when he declares himself ready to spill his own blood for those who will support him, Claudius is ready to say more. At just this moment, as if fated, a very different noise is heard from off stage. Both King and Queen fall silent and probably stand unmoving because they know who is about to enter.

156–71　Laertes changes as soon as he sees the 'madness' of his sister, both thoughts and sight becoming unbearable. Perhaps averting his eyes, he swears 'by heaven' to seek justice and recompense, and only then addresses Ophelia in gentle and loving terms.

She may approach him, turn away, or be entirely absorbed in her own silent mourning (as described at lines 6–13, above). Or he may go to her and grasp hold of her, to no avail; she makes no verbal response and may give no other sign of recognizing him, even though, before leaving the stage after her earlier entry, she had been determined to unburden herself to her 'brother' (l. 70, above). Recognition between near kin, after bereavement or forced separation, is the occasion for some of the most affecting scenes of all drama; this failure of brother and sister to recognize each other, when it seems that they must, can be deeply moving in performance, beyond the power of the words spoken.

When Ophelia has sung of a burial and said farewell to her 'dove' (possibly addressed to her brother), Laertes is more deeply moved than by any thought of revenge (see ll. 170–1).

172–87　From now on, Ophelia's second 'mad scene' is distinguished from the first by the contact she makes with those on stage – with Laertes, Claudius, Gertrude and, possibly, Horatio or whoever has been keeping 'good watch' over her (l. 74, above). But no one speaks to her, not even her brother, who has to assure himself of what he is witnessing and seek confirmation from others (l. 201).

Traditional associations of the flowers and herbs that Ophelia distributes (or imagines that she does) would give more knowledgeable persons in the audience a clearer indication of her thoughts and feelings than her speeches but the early texts give no indication to whom each one is given or what responses are made.

She has no flowers for a last gift of violets but her very next words are about a 'bonny sweet' love who is all her joy. As elsewhere in

these last appearances, both Hamlet and Polonius possess her imagination and the crazed 'thoughts and remembrances' of her songs and
speeches.

187–200   The last comment from Laertes, turning back to verse,
requires Ophelia's madness to be both frighteningly passionate and
affectingly tender: in effect, it should have a strange beauty and
attraction.

The second stanza of her last song is clearly about her father but
its first stanza is about someone unnamed who does not 'come
again', and may be a 'remembrance' of the Valentine whom she had
imagined coming to her bed in the last song of her previous scene –
and he might well have been Hamlet.

Prayers in the last line of the song and in the words spoken as she
leaves the stage are a new element introduced here. New too is the
call to 'Go to thy deathbed' (l. 193). These passages have led many
Ophelias to end their performance with a premonition of their own
death, some of them with a resolve to commit suicide. In these cases
she will include herself in the final prayer.

201–19   In many if not most performances Gertrude follows
Ophelia off stage, since it is she who will bring news of her death.
Horatio, if on stage, and any other attendants will probably leave at
the same time because what Claudius is about to say to Laertes
requires absolute privacy.

Once alone, Claudius is firm ('I must . . .') and open ('wisest
friends' can judge what he says). He even puts his crown on the line
in order to help Laertes. Once Laertes has agreed, he promises to
execute whoever killed his father (l. 218) – he knows that this is
Hamlet – and they go off stage together. At this quiet moment of
agreement, an audience that does not know the play will be in doubt
about the ways in which both the revenge stories will develop.

Act IV, scene vi

This fifth short scene in the seven scenes of this Act presents a crucial
development in the action and, by concentrating attention on the

absent Hamlet, counterbalances the focus of the previous, far longer scene. The contrast is accentuated by the arrival of 'seafaring men', who are strangers to Elsinore, and by reading out important facts from a letter in prose. All this happens in a few lines and the audience is left to make its own conclusions.

1–12 Hamlet has ensured that his letter is delivered to the one person he can absolutely trust. Horatio takes it without comment and probably moves apart to read it. Secrecy and danger are both present.

13–33 Hamlet has been careful in choosing what he risks setting down, and sends two messengers when one might be thought sufficient. He asks Horatio to join him as promptly and speedily as if he were fleeing '*death*' (l. 23) and then, with a quibble on 'light', reveals nothing more. Horatio is likely to change the way he reads while he is reading, concern changing to pleasure and a willingness to follow instructions; he may be apprehensive and puzzled as he finishes. He does not stop to thank the message bearers.

Act IV, scene vii

Having witnessed the pain of Ophelia and Laertes, the audience is now drawn into the suffering of Claudius as he and Laertes plan what to do. Although often, and indeed usually, performed in a shortened version (the texts of Q1 and F show how this may be done), in the text of Q2 this encounter is longer than any other in the play except that of Gertrude and Hamlet in Act III. The talk is neither so passionate nor so varied as that between mother and son, nor do these two differ in the outcome they seek, but as Claudius leads Laertes from anger and grief to action and deceit, he reveals a knowledge of himself and others that bears numerous signs of first-hand and painful experience.

Gertrude's report of Ophelia's off-stage death stops all other concerns, with a return of very palpable distress. The repetition of 'drowned' (ll. 164–5 and 183–4) and the tears (see ll. 185–91) express feelings that have overflowed the bounds of speech. As the tragedy moves towards its last Act, members of an audience are left to watch, with few words to guide or sustain their feelings: the effect can be numbing.

1–29 Claudius has already told Laertes that his father was killed by Hamlet, and has shared his fear of being the next victim. He speaks as a 'friend' (l. 2) but has not told the whole story, as Laertes recognizes. Suspicion and uneasiness remain between them. His two answers to Laertes' question supply personal and then political motives for his actions and both are concerned with the love that others have for Hamlet. He admits uncertainty and insecurity (see ll. 10–11, 13, and 21–4) and, with regard to Gertrude, a sense of exclusion (ll. 11–16). He ends with an incomplete verse-line where a pause can show Laertes either waiting for more information or working out the implications of what he has been told. He then replies with contrasting certainty and what amounts to a pledge to work independently if necessary.

30–5 Recognizing that his words have not satisfied Laertes – he may be more agitated than before – Claudius still does not tell the whole truth. With a self-deprecating metaphor, he promises a fuller explanation but – as an audience knows well – he fails to say that he has already arranged that Hamlet will be killed in England. Ironically, the murderer talks of 'love' (l. 34), as he had in his previous speech: the actor will have to find what emphasis to give the word – whether love is the 'virtue' or the 'plague' of Claudius.

36–51 Several details in the delivery of the letters are odd. Nothing had been said in the previous scene about one addressed to Gertrude. Claudio is a name not mentioned elsewhere and may have been used to hide Horatio's involvement in the business. Claudius had been expecting to hear of Hamlet's death and yet he invites Laertes to hear his letter before he has checked its content. Together these details give a strained and suspicious tone to this short episode. Then, for some unspoken reason, the King turns for advice to Laertes, who knows nothing of the fate intended for Hamlet: this may show the extent of his bewilderment and, possibly, a renewed fear.

50–108   When he is assured that Laertes can be trusted to kill Hamlet, Claudius begins to unfold a detailed plan as if he had, all the time, had it ready for such a contingency. By line 105, Laertes is impatient to get to the point and yet Claudius still hesitates, yet again questioning Laertes' resolve – he responds by almost bluntly asking why (l. 108).

The emotional tempo and physical bearing of the young man will be very different from those of the experienced and troubled regicide. The contrasting dynamics can become very clear in performance: Laertes, perhaps, unable to stay still; Claudius unmoving but looking away at times, lost in thoughts of his own weakness or failure.

This passage is among those cut for performance from earliest times (see pp. 6–8, above) but recent productions have shown that the full text of Q2 can hold attention and mark a significant and affecting stage in the journey of Claudius through the play.

109–22   Before getting to the 'quick o'th'ulcer' (l. 122) – in other words, to the 'hectic' in his own blood (IV.iii.68) – Claudius speaks, very personally, of his own experience of love: 'I think . . . I know . . . I see . . .'). His tone of voice and the focus of attention will change as he admits his growing estrangement from Gertrude (see her silence, as noted, at IV.i.29ff., and her lone exit, as noted at IV.v.201): the 'very flame of love' has become his 'plague' (ll. 113 and 13, above).

The Folio omits Shakespeare's delicate and sustained handling of Claudius in his suffering: after line 112, its text goes straight to 'Hamlet comes back' (l. 123). But, whether spoken or not, these thoughts inform the text later in the play: see, for example, the rare and loving epithet of 'How, sweet Queen' (l. 162), the unheeded calls for her to 'follow' (ll. 191–3) with which this scene closes, and her independence from Claudius at Ophelia's graveside and in the final scene.

123–47   With reflection over and Laertes ready to commit sacrilege to avenge his father, Claudius at last lays out his plan in full. He speaks directly now and Laertes answers in much the same manner when he reveals the steps he has already taken. His revenge contrasts with Hamlet's in cunning as well as recklessness.

147–61   Claudius is still not satisfied until he has thought of a back-up for both their plans, a third cunning and secret means of death. He may seem lacking in confidence and fearful of failure or, in a Machiavellian and ruthless performance, he can positively enjoy his own cunning.

Laertes waits in silence for Claudius to work out the plan, either restless and impatient (see 'Soft' [*wait, stay*], l. 153) or standing by patiently, his mind settled, and so making the insecurity of Claudius more apparent to an audience.

161–83   Gertrude's entrance brings a huge and sudden change of mood: her first words identify the change of feeling and then, as briefly as possible, tell the news. The incomplete verse-line 165 indicates a pause before or during Laertes' brief reply, in which astonishment, grief, and incomprehension can all be appallingly present. As if to cover her own deep feeling, Gertrude answers his question very precisely at first, before she slowly recaptures her experience in a carefully detailed description.

For the actor, this 'Willow speech' is both a difficult technical challenge in phrasing, articulation, and projection and a wonderful opportunity to lay bare Gertrude's deep sorrow while avoiding almost all direct expression of it. Absorbed and alone in her recollection, she can seem unable to escape from her 'woe' while the presence of Laertes necessitates speech. Sustained by these two impulses, the picture of Ophelia's off-stage death becomes increasingly complete. The forward pressure of the play's action is held back so that the imagination of audience members can share in Ophelia's death and respond to emblems of vernal innocence and the account of ancient traditions: familiar tunes may be half-heard in memory. This extraordinary feat of dramaturgy has given Gertrude's speech a life beyond the limits of the play, in storytelling, visual art, and fantasies.

183–94   Laertes' response and Gertrude's single repeated word accompany grief rather than finding expression for it. When he speaks again his words are almost bathetically obvious and clumsily apologetic as he struggles to restrain his tears. At line 191 he leaves the stage precipitately, as if needing to be alone.

Claudius, once more afraid of consequences, leaves immediately afterwards. In contrast to all his other exits at the end of a scene, he has no couplet here: his last words call a second time for Gertrude to go with him. This will focus attention on her as she leaves the stage without speaking: an audience will note how soon or how willingly she goes, and whether she is weeping inconsolably or is now quite impassive, all feeling spent.

ACT V

Act V, scene i

With the return of Hamlet now imminent, talk of Christian burial and the digging of a grave prepare the audience for the end of the tragedy and yet, at the same time, take the action away from the Court into territory that will be familiar to any spectator who has been in a graveyard or seen two clowns perform in a theatre.

When Hamlet and Horatio enter they do not talk of revenge or treachery but listen as the gravedigger–Clown sings of youthful love, and watch as he throws up a skull from beneath the stage. Dramatic tension has been dissipated and narrative put on hold while the tragic hero is shown as an intelligent, questioning individual facing the fact of death and talking of an ordinary society that seeks possession and power by any possible means. He speaks in prose, not verse, and as much in jest as in earnest.

After this surprising and lengthy intermission, the play's action springs again into very varied life: a fight in or alongside the grave and Hamlet in a 'towering passion' (V.ii.75–80).

1–60 All three early texts call the gravedigger and his assistant 'Clowns' and the manner of their talk is close to that of popular comedians of every age. The citing of authorities, listing of possibilities, assertion and counter assertion, class-consciousness and specialist knowledge, confidence and puzzlement are all much used by clowns to animate performance and raise laughter while reflecting the concerns and prejudices of the time. Here, however, the talk is not free ranging but fixed on death, salvation, and judgement.

At lines 15–16, the First Clown probably demonstrates his point by representing 'the man' by a bone taken from the grave and the 'water' by a spadeful of earth and so, in effect, creating a puppet play-within-the-play. By representing the act of suicide in this slow and methodical way, Shakespeare has brought the off-stage death of Ophelia back into focus without telling the audience whether she has 'drowned herself wittingly' or not (ll. 12–13): a mystery remains.

In present-day performances the laboured wit of the riddles and an ingrained pessimism are likely to register without their original reference to death on the gallows as punishment for petty crimes (see p. 27, above).

61–70   In contrast to the Penguin and other editions, F directs Hamlet to enter with Horatio '*afar off*' after line 55. This gives him time to hear the Clown singing of the incomparable pleasure of youthful love, so that his first comment (ll. 65–6) may be a reflection on his own state of mind compared with that of a gravedigger. Commenting on the second verse (ll. 76–7), he is more obviously conscious of his own predicament since he remembers Cain who, like Claudius, had killed his own brother, a parallel that the murderer has already made (see III.iii.36–8).

The gravedigger changes and mangles the widely accepted version of a ballad entitled 'The Aged Lover Renounceth Love'. His version of the first stanza takes pleasure in the memory of youthful love instead of the usual opening, 'I loathe that I did love, / In youth that I thought sweet.' The ballad was sufficiently popular that early audiences may have noticed this modification, which makes it more relevant to the 'honey' of Hamlet's vows to Ophelia (III.i.157).

71–115   Skulls and, probably, bones (see l. 90) casually tossed out of the grave cause Hamlet to remember the 'uses of this world' (I.ii.134) that charge his thoughts elsewhere in the play, both before and after this moment of reflection, as he returns to take revenge on Claudius. As he speaks of a murderer, politician, courtier, lawyer and speculator, all characterized with humorous asperity, some Hamlets laugh mordantly at their own wit. Others take this passage lightly, using the description of others to keep thoughts of their own death at bay.

Some struggle as they try to move laughter 'in the throat of death' (*Love's Labour's Lost*, V.ii.841) or become a fellow clown with the gravedigger.

Believing that Horatio is not 'passion's slave', Hamlet may be trying to tame his own mind when he turns to him for corroboration. Horatio says nothing to contradict him but his comments seem intended to restrain his friend's excesses, as they had done after *The Mousetrap* (see III.ii.182 and 294): they probably stand close together facing the grave, with Horatio holding a little back.

115–39   As he will admit to his friend (ll. 135–6), Hamlet's wit has become more aggressive and more resilient in talking with the Clown–gravedigger. Breaking off the engagement, with a mild oath he thinks back over the last three years and sees how the 'uses of the world' ignore established order in society, the weaker threatening the more powerful. Alternatively, Hamlet may be making a joke against himself by admitting that the 'peasant' (i.e., the Clown) has 'galled' him by making him think about where he is going: this would motivate his turning back to the gravedigger.

From lines 128–32 the audience may gather that Horatio has not told Hamlet of Ophelia's madness and death. At present the grave reminds him of every person's mortality, including his own. The Clown's 'quick lie' (ll. 126–7) may give Hamlet (and the audience) a premonition that his own death is imminent. This thought can surface into words when Hamlet realizes that their talk may 'undo' them; perhaps this causes him to change the subject quickly.

141–61   Hamlet's new line of questioning brings the talk still closer to himself. He does not comment when this unknown man says he started to work as a gravedigger on the day of his father's defeat of Fortinbras, but when he goes on to say that this was the very day when 'young Hamlet was born', 'Ay, marry' (l. 147) may follow a moment of silence in which he senses the hand of fate in the improbable coincidence. The Clown's two jokes about England and madness are sure to bring laughter in the theatre and dispel deeper thoughts until, with a change of subject, he volunteers the information that he started digging graves thirty years ago: this still further emphasizes the coincidence of their meeting by correctly implying Hamlet's age (see pp. 3–4, above).

As if seeking to escape from the ominous suggestion that this man, accidentally encountered, has spent a lifetime in readiness to dig his grave, Hamlet starts a more general line of enquiry. Alternatively, Hamlet may have accepted the fatefulness and is now thinking of his own body after it has been laid 'i'th'earth' (l. 161). Either way, the gravedigger–Clown appears to have entered the play at this moment to mark Hamlet as his victim, like those skeletal representatives of Death in allegorical Morality plays or visual depictions of the 'Dance of Death'. Hamlet, in turn, begins to function as 'Everyman'; he may even acknowledge this with his question about 'a man' at line 161.

162–81   The Clown's answers stay close to matters that concern Hamlet: first, the corrupt currents of the world (see Commentary, ll. 115–39, above) and then Ophelia's watery death – he will not recognize the relevance of this, but some in the audience might. When he picks up Yorick's skull and speaks of twenty-three years ago, he awakens Hamlet's lively memories of a time when he was seven years old, as becomes clear almost immediately (see l. 183, below).

When naming Yorick, the gravedigger may hand the skull to Hamlet, who in response, by the time he says 'This?' (an exclamation or question), may look it in the face. Alternatively, Hamlet may be so moved by his memories that he delays taking the skull until 'Let me see' (l. 181).

For an audience, if not for Hamlet, the further coincidence of this being Yorick's skull will strengthen the impression that some Fate or Providence is at work or that the gravedigger is a personification of Death and his clown's role a means of making its presence felt. At least, his unexpected arrival in the tragedy has, by now, widened the audience's focus of attention to include the whole of Hamlet's life, and encouraged its expectation that eventually, like a player, he will 'tell all' (III.ii.150–1). For early audiences, the Clown has also related the action of the play to their own lives and to topical issues.

182–92   Like the Queen's 'Willow speech', Hamlet's reaction to Yorick's skull has had a life of its own outside the bounds of the play.

The jester's name is now a byword that links folly with both affection and death. This one speech 'unkennels' (III.ii.91) Hamlet's capacity for enjoyment and admiration, without diminishing his horror of death and distrust of the 'paint' that others use in order to face the world (l. 190; see also, III.i.143–5).

At first, Hamlet reacts instinctively with 'Alas, poor Yorick', and then his memory takes over with particular recollections that collide with his horrified 'imagination', which is described so tangibly ('My *gorge* rises at it. . . . *Here* hung those lips that I have *kissed* . . .') that the actor's performance is likely to be physically changed.

In this context and at this stage in the narrative, a few words and the actor's very presence can give an impression of deep feeling. Actors whose interpretation of the role is intellectual and sceptical, rather than romantic and affecting, can use this speech to continue the harsh humour from earlier in the scene and the passionate denunciations of women from earlier in the play. An aggressive interpretation can make a mockery of affection and the efforts of 'jest' and 'fancy'. In less troubled performances, actors can address the skull held out in a single hand as if it were Yorick himself and then move its jaw, with Hamlet ventriloquizing, when Yorick is sent off to visit 'my lady'. In this way the speech becomes a comic puppet play-within-the-play, as the gravedigger–Clown had used the bones a short time ago (see Commentary on lines 1–60).

The extent to which Hamlet speaks to himself, forgetting Horatio, is another question for actors: the speech can develop into an involuntary and disorientating soliloquy.

192–212   With the gentler, perhaps apologetic, 'Prithee,' Hamlet turns to Horatio to ask his opinion. Thoughts of decaying flesh and 'my lady's' deception have led him to think of a great and youthful hero who lived in ancient times. Instead of providing an escape from his present predicament, these thoughts bring him back to himself (see l. 199) and then on to Julius Caesar, all-conquering and, eventually, assassinated. In his 'imagination' he considers their fates (ll. 199–209) and, although he does not use these words at this time, in the 'image' of their deaths he 'sees the portraiture' of his own (V.ii.77–8).

This contemplative passage can draw an audience to empathize with Hamlet as he stands on the brink of a grave, watched silently by a gravedigger–Clown and sharing his thoughts with a trusted and learned friend. As if aware that he could become merely fanciful or morbid, he illustrates his meaning with the mundane bung of a 'beer barrel' and either improvises or quotes in rhymed verse.

When Hamlet had last left the stage, he resolved that his 'thoughts' would be 'bloody, or be nothing worth' (IV.iv.65–6) but he has been deflected from that purpose by affection for Yorick and thoughts of his own death. Then, at this very moment, his father's murderer, his mother, and the whole Court enter silently in Ophelia's funeral procession: action calls and Fate again seems to be at work.

212–18 The sound of a bell (see l. 230) will draw the audience's attention before the slow procession arrives on stage so that Hamlet has time to speak before stepping aside at line 218. The familiar persons who now fill the stage are dressed in mourning clothes and changed in bearing. Attended by the markedly new figure of a priest, they settle silently in appropriate places around the grave in which Ophelia's body is to be laid to rest.

219–50 Four very different activities start simultaneously and continue, each in its own and mostly slow tempo:

(1) Preparations are made for the burial, supervised by the Priest.
(2) Gertrude steps apart to strew flowers over the grave.
(3) Hamlet watches from the side and is now silent, except to identify Laertes, son of the man he has killed.
(4) Laertes repeatedly questions the ceremony and, when the Priest insists that it is the fullest permissible, speaks of his sister as a 'ministering angel' (l. 237) and curses Hamlet.

While much of this is still happening, formality is disrupted when, unexpectedly and at a late moment, Laertes '*leaps*' into the open grave. He then embraces Ophelia, who must be lying in an open coffin, and asks, in hyperbolic and grandly mythological terms, to be buried with her. Both the dialogue and a stage direction (found in Q1 and F) call for this action, which can scarcely be anything but shocking and to some degree violent. If Laertes lifts Ophelia's unresisting body up into the view of everyone present, the effect can also be clumsy and grotesque.

250–63 Hamlet's four-line sentence as he approaches the grave is composed and coldly, almost humorously, objective; by implication, it is also dismissive. In contrast, the self-identification that follows is impressively brief; so too is his first reply to Laertes' curse (ll. 254–5).

The dialogue indicates that Laertes initiates the unarmed fight that follows by clutching at Hamlet's throat (see ll. 256 and 259). By the time Claudius orders 'Pluck them asunder' both are engaged in a close, physical struggle in which no one is able to intervene until, somehow, Horatio makes himself heard.

Such a fight at the side of an open grave would be dangerous for the actors and that may be the reason why Q1 has the stage direction '*Hamlet leaps in after Laertes*' and why an elegy on Richard Burbage, the first Hamlet, remembers 'Oft have I seen him leap into the grave.' Hand-to-hand fighting could be managed more safely on the solid bottom of the grave and half-concealed from the theatre audience. Yet separating the assailants inside the grave would involve other difficulties: a simpler way of staging the fight is to have Laertes, who is the aggressor, come out of the grave in order to grapple with Hamlet and this, despite the early stage directions, is what usually happens today.

264–9 By addressing him as 'my son', not Hamlet as at line 260, Gertrude makes a more personal and intimate appeal. His reply shows that, for a moment, she has regained the hard-won relationship established at the end of the closet scene (III.iv). They are both responsive to each other's presence.

The incomplete line of the Queen's intervention indicates a pause before Hamlet replies. Or, possibly, he replies at once, completing her verse-line, and then pauses before addressing Laertes. Either way, the stark simplicity of 'I loved Ophelia,' spoken for the first time as she lies dead before him, adds weight and prominence to this public declaration. Spoken by a prince and out of context, the words would have been almost incredible for early audiences (see I.iii.1–44 and 105–36, together with Commentary on II.ii.33–96).

With 'Forty thousand brothers' Hamlet returns to the hyperbole with which he responded to Laertes' rhetoric. Ineffective interventions from Claudius and Gertrude suggest that violent passion is about to return.

270–80 As Hamlet continues to challenge his adversary by offering to 'outface' his violence and ranting, the very energy of his utterance is liable to make him seem 'mad' (see ll. 268 and 280). The actor can choose (or discover in each performance) whether this is a conscious choice over which Hamlet exercises control, an instinctive surge of passion, or a return to an incipient madness that has occurred before, especially in the 'nunnery scene' with Ophelia (see Commentary at I.v.112–20; II.ii.205–37; and III.i.134–50). However it is played, the moment alarms and alerts everyone present.

280–8 Using the gentle image of a female dove, Gertrude (and she alone) is able to calm Hamlet so that his next words are reasonable and considerate to Laertes. The effort that this has involved leads him to leave the stage immediately afterwards. He says 'it is no matter ' but then issues a barely concealed challenge to Claudius in a concluding couplet: the fire within him is sustained and banked-down under its savage mockery. This exit can be as startling, in its own ominous way, as his fighting at the graveside or his declaration of love for Ophelia (l. 265) when he is too late to save her.

The Queen's speech beginning at line 280 is ascribed to the King in F and Q1. Nevertheless, very few editors have adopted this arrangement, which is at odds with how the action has developed and with Claudius's part in it. The Folio text also leaves Gertrude without an effective speech near the end of a scene in which she has had a considerable, if not crucial, influence. Q1 recognizes the need for a further contribution from Gertrude by giving her two speeches after Hamlet has left the stage, the second bringing the scene to its conclusion with a prayer to God for reconciliation with Laertes.

289–95   Once Hamlet has gone, Claudius takes centre-stage deci-sively. Each verse-line he speaks is a separate unit as he addresses the principal persons in turn and commits himself to immediate action.

Believing that the living Hamlet is about to be killed, Laertes might appreciate an irony in 'a living monument'. For an audience familiar with the play, 'An hour of quiet' can refer ironically to the time when its leading persons will all be dead; someone familiar with the text may hear it as a premonition of Hamlet's last words (see V.ii.352).

Act V, scene ii

After dangerous and passionate action on a crowded stage, a long duologue, interrupted by a challenge, requires the audience's close attention before the dramatic focus widens once more to encompass the whole stage. In this demanding way, preparation is made for the tragedy's culmination.

1–70   Except for the handing over of a royal commission to be read 'at more leisure' (l. 26), the opening text specifies no physical action or movement but its performance does need very precise thought and clear speaking. Played with a light and inner energy Hamlet's new confidence will hold an audience's attention, as well as Horatio's. For this account of what happened while he was absent from Denmark, the two friends have met privately in the main 'hall' at Elsinore (ll. 170 and 193) where the king gives public audiences, but they are not relaxed for long as their talk becomes, by turns, rapid, careful, humorous, hard-hitting, decisive, and reflective.

Hamlet starts thoughtfully, seeing a 'divinity', or providence, in recent events (an echo, perhaps, of the biblical *Proverbs*, XVI: 9 and an idea that recurs at line 48), but soon incredulity catches fire in short bursts of feeling: 'Ah, royal knavery! . . . With, ho! such bugs . . . No, not to stay . . .' (ll. 19, 22 and 24). When Horatio responds in the same way – 'Why, what a king is this!' (l. 62) – it prompts Hamlet to speak of his personal responsibility. Although phrased in a series of questions, what he says now builds impressively in syntax, metre and rhythm, through impassioned and clear-sighted denunciation, towards a twice-repeated acceptance of the moral duty to revenge (ll. 67–70).

Hamlet's new resolve is made all the more impressive for following immediately after his almost casual account of sending Rosencrantz and Guildenstern to a 'sudden death' (see ll. 38–47). When Horatio returns to this peremptory decision, Hamlet's response is almost impatient: 'Why, man, they did make love to this employment. / They are not near my conscience' (ll. 57–62). A lack of feeling for them also grows out of his sense that all events, including this act of rough justice, had become inevitable: 'There's a divinity that shapes our ends, / Rough-hew them how we will' (ll. 10–11).

Although nothing outwardly spectacular happens during this duologue, attention can be held by its narrative interest and by the variety of thought that underlies and motivates its words. A series of short verse-lines indicate pauses or short silences that encourage a close focus in which physical and nervous performance is able to attract attention and give expression to what remains unspoken.

71–80   After a pause or longer silence while Hamlet thinks of the future, Horatio brings him back to the present moment (ll. 71–2) and once again he is alert. In the two short statements of a single verse-line, he prepares to take charge of events but, unable to *do* anything at this moment of decision, he continues to reflect on his predicament, speaking first of the brevity of all lives (l. 74) – perhaps foreseeing his own imminent death – and then of events at Ophelia's burial, regretting his own 'towering passion' (l. 80).

The passion shown by Laertes at the graveside has led Hamlet to see in him a reflection of his own 'cause' [*motive, obligation*] to avenge his father's death. For an audience this recognition can identify the 'grief' within Hamlet as he prepares to take revenge; for him, it may strengthen the sense of being led by circumstances, as if 'heaven' or 'destiny' were shaping his 'ends' (ll. 10 and 48, above). He is so occupied with these thoughts that Horatio has to warn him of Osrick's approach.

81–105   The entrance of Osrick springs as great a surprise as that of the two Clowns at the start of the previous scene. At this late and tense moment in the play's action, someone not seen or mentioned before has joined the cast. He is said to be 'young' (see l. 192, below), as are Hamlet, Laertes, Rosencrantz and Guildenstern, and Fortinbras, but his effusive and elaborate speech immediately shows him to be unlike any other person in the play.

By provoking the audience's laughter in a serious situation, Osrick functions as the gravedigger–Clown had done. His handling of a hat, like the Clown's tossing up of bones and skulls, introduces visual comedy and sight-gags (see ll. 93–101 and 176–7). Hamlet responds much as he did to the gravedigger, by commenting on Osrick's way of life and echoing his manner of speech. Obviously, there are big differences too – Osrick is called a 'waterfly' and 'lapwing' (ll. 83 and 182), not an 'ass' and 'mad knave' (V.i.78 and 99) – but his exchanges with Hamlet, like the Clown's, bring the play closer to an audience's own life-experiences with talk of privileged birth, abuse of wealth, and misuse or guile in the use of language.

90–105 By talking with Horatio, Hamlet has kept Osrick silent before he can say why he has entered and, now that he has regained attention, Hamlet keeps him waiting by drawing attention to his manners. Taking a cue from lines 176–7, Osrick usually makes an elaborate 'flourish' with his hat, which is often extravagantly feathered or extremely large. To amuse himself or because he is suspicious of this visitor's intentions, Hamlet then delays him still further with disagreement about the weather.

Perhaps Hamlet and Horatio have moved away from Osrick and he has used his hat to draw their attention but, as soon as Osrick mentions 'his majesty' (l. 91), Hamlet becomes more wary and alert. Very probably, his subsequent treatment of this messenger is his way of testing how readily he has taken instruction and how willing he is to change his mind. After hearing of the 'great wager' on his head (l. 102) Hamlet gives Osrick time to say whatever he chooses and thereby show his true colours.

Osrick can be played as an amusing and inconsequential caricature but the actor will know (and at this point a reader should take note) that he is clever enough and sufficiently trusted by Claudius to be put in charge of the duel. He must be able to ensure that Laertes takes the unbated and envenomed rapier. Later he will be fully advised of the arrival of Fortinbras and the English Ambassadors.

Such a person could only pretend to be a fool – and Osrick might have chosen to do just that as a way of hiding the treachery and danger of the duel.

The degree to which those on stage are aware of tension and danger, or how much Hamlet enjoys baiting Osrick, will depend on the individual actors or their director. It might be possible to play the text so that all laughs are avoided or killed as they are about to start but that would be difficult to sustain, and would lose the advantages of a relief from tension before the emotionally demanding end of the tragedy.

106–31   The Folio text and many productions omit this passage so that Osrick jumps from 'Sir' to 'You are not ignorant . . .'. This is not an easy transition for the actor to make unless some business is introduced with the hat or Osrick betrays signs of unease.

This further talk of duelling would have raised the dramatic temperature at a time when resort to swords was not uncommon as a means of settling disputes without recourse to the processes of justice. Duelling according to strict rules (see, for example, *Romeo and Juliet*, II.iii.17–24) was a popular spectator sport that often took place in London theatres but, although officially forbidden, it was also a way of defending or restoring a gentleman's honour (see, for example, *As You Like It*, V.iii.46–101). As they spar, with words instead of swords, Osrick hesitates twice and for long enough to allow Horatio to intervene.

132–69   When Osrick reaches the nub of his message, Hamlet asks, simply and directly, 'How if I answer no?' (l. 167), which brings confirmation of the danger that has underlain all their talk: 'I mean, my lord, the opposition of your person in trial.' Hamlet has been keeping 'an eye of him', as he had of Rosencrantz and Guildenstern before he led them to confess their hidden purpose (II.ii.290). Now that Osrick has been brought to his 'trial', the 'bubbles' of his wit burst (ll. 189–90, below) and, very soon, keeping what 'state' he can in his exit (*Love's Labour's Lost*, V.ii.588), he leaves the stage.

170–90   Coolly and carefully, in short and simple phrases, Hamlet accepts what he knows is a trap. Once Osrick has gone, he reflects bitterly and at some length on this courtier and the 'drossy age' that he knows well (ll. 185–6) and that his first audiences could recognize as their own: his mind reaches out from the particular to its widest implications.

191–202 F's deletion of this passage and its stage direction is nearly always followed in performance (and in some recent editions) because it adds little to the narrative and delays the play's conclusion. Reasons for retaining it and, perhaps, for Shakespeare writing it are:

(1) When Claudius sends for confirmation, Hamlet knows for sure that the duel will be a crucial 'trial' (l. 165, above). His answer slyly mocks the King's uncertainty.

(2) The Queen's request for 'gentle entertainment' towards Laertes reminds Hamlet of his outburst of passion; perhaps, also, of her intervention that had quietened him (see V.i.280–4).

(3) Here, without the diversionary eccentricity of Osrick, Hamlet is shown to be 'constant' and 'ready' (ll. 195–6), and responsive to his mother.

(4) Immediately before the momentary demands of the final encounters, a 'breathing time of day' (l. 171) is established after which Hamlet will soon speak calmly of his present predicament in the context of his whole life.

203–17 Horatio's fear of the outcome changes the audience's view of Hamlet before he speaks of all that is 'ill' about his heart and then, as before (see I.ii.85 and III.ii.373–4), pulls back from such 'foolery', adding only that it is 'such a kind of gain-giving as would perhaps trouble a woman'. Those words are ambiguous and tell the audience very little: is he thinking of his mother or Ophelia, or is this very general reference another way of admitting his own weakness and cowardice?

The specific references in Hamlet's next and more sustained speech are unique in this and all of Shakespeare's tragedies. Borrowing from Christ's Sermon on the Mount in St Matthew's Gospel, X: 29, the revenging hero quotes a text that Calvin and popular preachers used when asserting that a 'special [*individual*] providence' shaped every human life – in other words, that God was responsible for the accidents of their lives. Hamlet then alludes to the traditional view that Christians should live each day in 'readiness' to die. Such an acceptance of death would have had further resonance in the stoicism of Seneca's *Epistles* and the scepticism of Montaigne's *Essays*.

This strongly placed and exceptional speech is a major challenge for the actor. Hamlet can either retreat into conventional attitudes or give the borrowed words a new force and personal validity. The repetitions can either call for slow and thoughtful speech, each word individually considered and weighted, or encourage a lighter tone that brushes aside Horatio's premonition of danger and doom. Perhaps Hamlet is seeking courage to face his own fears by defying 'augury' (compare *Macbeth*, V.v.44–50). Alternatively, from 'I shall win at the odds' onwards (l. 205), he could be boasting before combat, as many heroes had done before him.

218   'Let be' can be spoken in many different ways, from a casual instruction to stand aside on hearing the King's approach (see Q1, 'Here comes the king'), to a thoughtful acceptance of danger or imminent death. (See also, p. 143, below.) The two words are found only in Q2: F omits them as if actors, author, or bookkeeper had found them ineffective; or, perhaps they were accidentally skipped or edited out in the printing-house.

218–21   As Hamlet and Horatio stand aside and the Court assembles once more, the audience's attention will shift markedly. Everything is likely to be carried out in good order and purposefully, nothing gaining close attention except, possibly, the rapiers and flagon of wine. When everyone is settled, Claudius brings the focus back to Hamlet who moves centre-stage and face-to-face with Laertes, who will be standing silent beside the King. The only other time they were this close together Laertes' hands had been at Hamlet's throat (see V.i.255–60). Speech no longer 'Conjures the wandering stars' (V.i.252): when the King puts Laertes' hand in his, Hamlet speaks reasonably and asks for pardon; Laertes remains silent. Almost certainly this is not what an audience will expect, or anyone on stage: underneath the gentlemanly behaviour the situation remains highly fraught.

222–48 Still troubled at heart and 'be-netted round with villainies' (ll. 206–7 and 29), Hamlet speaks in the 'presence' of the Court with the finesse of a duellist and man of honour. Laertes replies in kind but the difficulties of this exchange are marked by two pauses (indicated by incomplete verse-lines) and Hanlet's unexpected answers to his own questions: 'Was't Hamlet . . . Who does it then?'

For everyone in the theatre audience and for the Queen, Hamlet's plea of 'madness' (l. 231) will be, at least, questionable, having heard him repeatedly deny that he was mad and watched his pretended madness. Only in a limited sense can he be speaking the truth: he recently told Horatio that to Laertes he had 'forgot' himself (ll. 75–80) and his behaviour then had similarities to his reactions on seeing the ghost, encountering Ophelia, and going to his mother's closet; then he seemed to have lost control of himself and been close to hysteria. A readiness to 'drink hot blood' (III.ii.397), for example, might well be called 'madness'. Hamlet's apology to Laertes touches on the most secret and mysterious parts of his own nature.

When Laertes answers in good form, all difficulties skipped over or forgotten – not least his own intention to kill Hamlet by dishonourable means – a theatre audience could scarcely miss the irony and deceit in speaking like 'a gentleman' (l. 221) and in 'terms of honour' (l. 240). Hamlet draws the exchange to an end briskly, even eagerly, speaking in the same vein.

248–60 Taking the foils and exchanging self-deprecating courtesies follow a routine course but the audience may focus on Laertes as he chooses the unbated and poisoned weapon: Osrick's role in making sure of this may come as a surprise that gives a sense that the contest has been more rigged than words have betrayed.

261–90 After Claudius has boosted the dignity of the occasion by dissolving a fabulous pearl in the wine, the audience's knowledge that the cup has now been poisoned greatly augments the thrills of well-matched opponents in a skilful game and 'trial'. For some spectators, 'destiny' may seem to be 'ordinant' (ll. 8–11 and 48) when Hamlet unthinkingly refuses the now-lethal drink. Gertrude's drinking as she 'carouses' to Hamlet's 'fortune' adds both tension and irony as the situation engulfs all the participants and widens the audience's attention.

Because Laertes and Claudius take this opportunity to speak aside it seems likely that Shakespeare intended Gertrude should go to Hamlet and wipe his face after he has refused to do it for himself (see ll. 288–90). If he is already prepared to resume the duel she will put herself in danger by stepping between the two opponents in order to care for her son as if he were still a child in her arms.

At this juncture physical actions and their consequences are likely to be the dominant elements of the play. So much is in the balance that words cannot compete and a fearful silence will pervade the stage. Much is left to the actors: how does Hamlet submit to his mother's care and how tender or satisfied is she? Or does he not react at all, his thoughts still on danger, honour, revenge, and the 'trial' he is undergoing?

291–302 The fight rapidly becomes 'incensed' (l. 296) so that the audience may not see how the rapiers are exchanged, as stage directions in both F and Q1 explain. Q2 gives no help here and fight directors in recent productions have managed it in many other ways that give Hamlet varying degrees of conscious intention, from murderous anger to fated acquiescence. The fight stops when both contestants are wounded and poisoned (see l. 301). Osrick, Horatio, and the King all intervene verbally but Hamlet speaks only of the Queen, his mother (l. 302).

302–16 The last contact between Gertrude and Hamlet will be played according to how their performances have developed throughout the play. Her repetitions can represent both urgent concern and a struggle against increasing pain and weakness. 'O my dear Hamlet' suggests that he is close to her now, perhaps holding her in his arms where she has fallen. What she says does not directly implicate Claudius, and Hamlet's subsequent 'Seek it out' implies that she does not even look at her husband: mother and son may be totally engaged with each other.

When Laertes accuses the King, Hamlet acts at once: he is physically and emotionally transformed and, in a moment, becomes both judge and avenger.

317–21   A striking element in the rapidly changing situation is that Claudius can do nothing and speaks to no effect. No 'friends' come to his aid when he calls and when he claims to be 'but hurt' he knows that he is fatally poisoned (see IV.vii.139–47). Although still at the centre of his Court, he is manifestly powerless: in a single line Hamlet denounces him on three separate counts and then, with a savage pun on *union*, poisons him a second time.

321–52   With vindication and an offer of forgiveness, Laertes starts a quieter development with Hamlet in command and Horatio at his side. Having exchanged forgiveness with his dying opponent and acknowledged the poison working in himself, Hamlet turns for the last time to his mother. In some productions he has already gone to her and 'Wretched Queen, adieu!' is then a public acknowledgement of deep personal loss. In most performances, however, this farewell is brief because he is more concerned that his revenge should be understood by the 'yet unknowing world' (l. 373): then these few words can seem to muffle his deep-set grief while emphasizing how much remains for him to do.

A short tussle to prevent his friend's suicide is followed by a call to 'God' and an earnest appeal to tell his story to the 'harsh world' (ll. 338–43). From line 328 onwards, Hamlet thinks repeatedly of the world and the 'time' he was born to 'set right' (I.v.188–9). It may be that the audience sees a new and calmer Hamlet, no longer engaged with the present. Repeatedly he insists that his work is done: 'I am dead, Horatio. . . . Horatio, I am dead. . . . O, I die, Horatio . . . the rest is silence.' For the future, he supports Fortinbras as King of Denmark.

Alternatively, Hamlet can accept death with a sense of frustration, rather than completion. So he wants his 'cause' truthfully reported (ll. 333–4) but is ready to see the throne of Denmark pass to a prince who sends soldiers to their deaths for an 'eggshell . . . a straw . . . a fantasy and trick of fame' (IV.iv.18–28 and 47–65). This

Hamlet has a clear-sighted (or cynical) belief that, where he has failed, clear decisions and ruthless authority may prevail.

Between these two possibilities lie many others. The arrival of Fortinbras is the last major surprise of the play and it comes at just the right moment, as if fated. Consequently Hamlet's support of his equally surprising claim to the throne may be an acceptance of heaven's ordering (V.ii.48), a prophecy (see l. 349) rather than a personal and responsible choice: in Shakespeare's day, holy men at their death were said to have 'good inspirations' (*Merchant of Venice*, I.ii.27–8; see also *Richard II*, II.i.31).

Perhaps at death Hamlet is chiefly concerned that the full extent of his 'cause' is made known to those who 'look pale and tremble at this chance' (l. 328) and is ready for silence and death when he is sure that Horatio will report the 'occurrents, more and less', of what will, by then, be Danish history.

Fortinbras, arriving in time to see nothing but the outcome of the action, sees the carnage as if it were a 'field' of battle (l. 396) and orders military honours for Hamlet. This is the last judgement that Shakespeare provided on his hero: the death of a potential king at the conclusion of a campaign. Before Fortinbras arrives, Horatio has given a wholly different assessment in the language of affection, chivalry, and religion (ll. 353–4).

352 (stage direction)   The manner of Hamlet's death has differed greatly in performance. Q2 has no stage direction at this point, Q1 has the direction '*Hamlet dies*' and F follows '*Dies*' with 'O, o, o, o', which a stage direction in the Oxford edition interprets as '*a long sigh*'. The Folio reading is typographically irregular and may be a late unauthorized addition to mark the time an actor took for Hamlet to die slowly and painfully as the 'potent poison' takes effect (ll. 347). More usually in practice today, Hamlet dies peacefully in Horatio's arms, 'Now cracks a noble heart' (l. 353) describing a physical failure that only he can identify.

A quiet death can contrast strongly with other deaths in this scene of carnage and with the 'drum' that announces the arrival of Fortinbras (l. 355). A protracted and painful one will add to the horror of a time when 'men's minds are wild' and more 'mischances' threaten (ll. 388–9); then death alone can offer 'felicity' (l. 341).

353–4   Horatio's farewell echoes 'rest' from Hamlet's last words and assumes the existence of an afterlife in accordance with the very first appearance of the Ghost. His 'Good night' envisions death as a sleep, as Hamlet had done much earlier (III.i.60–3); his 'noble heart' and 'sweet prince' are in accord with Ophelia's recollection of him before the events of the tragedy (see III.i.151–61). Although out of key with the rest of the final scene, Horatio's tribute brings a sense of cyclical completion to the tragedy and, perhaps, of fulfilment, however slight such impressions may be. Talk of 'flights of angels' is a more personal fantasy that is unexpected from a student-philosopher (but thoughts of angels occur elsewhere in the course of the tragedy; see I.iv.39; III.iii.69; and V.i.237).

Horatio's two verse-lines have every appearance of a well-placed and considered counter statement to the terrors, passions, and political issues of the revenge story. In performance, with a strong Horatio, they can deeply affect the audience's response to the tragedy, a reaction that Horatio's leading part in the remaining minutes of the play can retain and develop in a wider context. In harsher, louder productions with Horatio played as an ineffectual friend – he has achieved little so far in the course of the story – his valediction will have little effect while the 'havoc' of the revenge story moves forward inexorably until the 'soldiers shoot' (ll. 358 and 397).

355–67   When action has come slowly, and probably quietly, to a halt, many more persons arrive on stage, marching to a drumbeat and carrying banners so that, with a jolt or shuddering, action starts again on a new tack. Questions follow, with the English Ambassador, a new entry to the play, filling in details of the story from elsewhere, until Horatio begins his task of reporting Hamlet's 'cause'. By now he will have risen from the side of his dead friend and everyone on stage and in the audience will wait on his words.

368 to the end   Everything seems set for irrefutable accusations and final judgements but Shakespeare did not write that speech.

Horatio speaks only in very general terms of 'unnatural acts' and blames what was 'accidental . . . casual . . . forced . . . mistook' (ll. 375–8). With those words and how he speaks them, or underneath them, Horatio is bound to show other feelings of love, sorrow, anger, frustration, longing for peace and rest, or whatever the actor's performance throughout the play dictates. Hamlet believed his chosen friend was 'not passion's slave', but now an audience will witness how feeling 'will out' (III.ii.82 and IV.vii.189) under the pressure of events; the 'search' is over (ll. 356–7).

As Fortinbras assumes control, the theatre audience is left to make its own judgement and supplement his assessment according to every individual's accumulated and personal experience of the tragedy. As all the bodies are taken up (see l. 395) and carried off stage with Hamlet's ahead of them, martial music and, according to the Folio, '*a peal of ordnance*' will both prolong the exit and cover any sound that may be made on stage or in the audience.

4 Key Productions and Performances

The Tragedy of Hamlet has two great strengths in performance: a sensational and affecting central role and a story with several strands and unexpected developments that holds attention from its very first moments until it ends with an awesome inevitability. The result has been a succession of packed and enthusiastic audiences starting with the play's earliest years and continuing with growing frequency until the present. It is now a reliable recourse and a constant challenge for all English-speaking theatres and for many others around the world, a staple of many repertoires and a reliable vehicle for launching new companies. After more than four hundred years, *Hamlet* remains a fixed star in the vast expanse of ever-changing theatrical possibilities. In more recent times, numerous films of *Hamlet* have been made.

Productions of all kinds stand or fall with the success of the exceptionally long central role. The play's most thrilling moments depend on Hamlet and, along the way, he seems to share his innermost thoughts with the audience whether he is alone on stage or engaged with whatever chance or opposition offers. Yet he also retains a mystery, as if moved by forces that work secretly and, sometimes, without his knowledge or consent. The role takes all that an actor can give: vivid sensation and quick intelligence; far-reaching imagination and complete physical identification with the man he plays. At full stretch the actor becomes Hamlet and with each new actor – sometimes with each new performance – the entire tragedy takes palpable form as never before. Having seen it played well, we want to see it again and see other productions with other actors as Hamlet.

As the Commentary of this Handbook shows, the play's narrative and central role draw strength and identifiable meanings from many reflections of everyday experience, the intellectual, political and social issues it raises, and the hero's contact with other persons on stage. It leaves such a broad and deep wake in the minds of audiences that the following account of its theatrical life concentrates on three key productions from the past, leaving films to represent more recent interpretations.

Betterton, Garrick, Macready, Kean, Kemble, and Booth

Greatly talented actors have emphasized different facets of the role and stamped it with their own personalities and yet almost all those actors have had one achievement in common. Thomas Betterton first played the role in 1661 when he was twenty-six years of age and continued to do so until 1709 when his performance was still that of 'a young man of great expectation, vivacity, and enterprise' (Richard Steele, *The Tatler*). Mental and physical energy are prime requirements for such a long role but in this play, as in others by Shakespeare, Betterton's rarer gift was to speak the text 'as if it had been written for him' (Nicholas Rowe, *Life of Shakespeare*): like that of many later actors, his Hamlet seemed to be alive upon the stage. David Garrick, who also played the role for many years, from 1742 to 1776, emphasized Hamlet's resolution and sensibility, the latter being a prized quality in art and culture of the time. His father's death gave purpose to this Hamlet's actions, and Garrick's expressions of fear on seeing the Ghost were strongly emphasized and frequently noted. This reading was carefully fostered: a special wig caused his hair to stand on end when he first saw the apparition and a chair would always collapse when he was startled by its reappearance in his mother's presence (Act III, scene iv). Both tricks worked for his audience because Garrick had so totally assumed the person he played; all his senses were engaged as if he was experiencing whatever the action demanded. Although performances of long ago can only be glimpsed through eyewitness reports, this fragmentary evidence shows that audiences would sometimes respond as if Hamlet were actually present before them and, at these moments, both theatre and actor would be forgotten.

So many actors played Hamlet over the course of many years that their audiences' belief in a 'young Hamlet' must have owed much to the actor's ability to awaken the imagination of audiences. Portraits of actors in the role and nineteenth-century photographs show us middle-aged and posturing gentlemen in costume rather than the person we know from reading the play or seeing a contemporary production and yet these Hamlets drew crowds to their perfor- mances. The 'young' Hamlet of the text has had a charmed life in the theatre as if custom cannot stale Shakespeare's invention and the age of the actor need not take its usual toll.

John Philip Kemble played Hamlet between 1783 and 1817, his thoughtful, noble and melancholic prince impressive in both speech and silent presence. Edmund Kean played a restless, passionate and tormented Hamlet from 1814, at the age of twenty-five, until shortly before his death in 1833. These two Hamlets were compared as if they were persons encountered in life: in William Hazlitt's words, 'Mr. Kean's Hamlet is as much too splenetic and rash as Mr. Kemble's is too delib- erate and formal' (*Characters of Shakespeare's Plays*, 1817). One actor was neo-classical and consistent, the other relied on momentary flashes and transitions between sharply contrasting feelings. As John Keats wrote in a letter of 14 August 1819, Kean had made a 'revolution' in acting when compared with his predecessors. William Charles Macready had played Hamlet many times but his success was not acknowledged until he was in his early forties, around 1835. Later he told a critic, John Marston, that 'no man ever played [Hamlet] with any approach to completeness until he was too old to look it'. He sought to express 'the impetuous rebellion of a generous nature when its trust has been cruelly deceived' and to follow this, in the last Act, with a new spirit of 'resignation'. These contrasts, he said, demanded passion, imagination, irony and what he called 'colloquial realism' (*Our Recent Actors*, 1890).

In the nineteenth century, notable Hamlets received long reviews that compared one with another and judged their 'colloquial realism' or emotional 'reality'. The 'Hamlet experience' given by Edwin Booth, the American actor, in the 1860s and 1870s, was described in detail and praised fulsomely in William Winter's *The Life and Art of Edwin Booth* (1893): 'His impersonation had wealth of emotion, exalted poetry of treatment, and a dream-like quality that could not fail to

fascinate; but, above all, when at its best, the terrible reality of suffering.' The contrasting emotions and sentiments of the role had 'found
their roots and springs in the being of the man. Booth seemed to live
Hamlet rather than to act it' (pp. 166 and 171).

Henry Irving

Henry Irving played Hamlet at the Lyceum Theatre in London from
1874 to 1885 in his own production. The tragedy was usually
performed in repertoire that included other less demanding plays but
in its first season this *Hamlet* had a run of two hundred nights, at that
time its longest consecutive life on the stage. Irving was both traditional and innovatory, studying earlier interpretations with great
care and yet setting his own mark on the role and the play. Before
long the production had won pride of place for the Lyceum among
London theatres. Its capacity had to be increased to meet growing
demand and its stage and lighting equipment and its army of supernumeraries and stagehands soon outclassed all competition. Irving
will be considered here as a prime example of how an actor–manager
in the role could control and dominate an audience's experience.

Fortunately for us, the great mass of evidence about Irving's
Hamlet has been sifted and carefully assessed by Alan Hughes in *Henry
Irving, Shakespearean* (1981) and the following account is indebted to its
chapter on *Hamlet*, the longest in the book. For an eyewitness
account of the early performances on which Irving's reputation was
founded, extensive use has been made of Edward R. Russell's *Irving as
Hamlet* (1875). This study by an intimate friend and close associate
from the actor's earliest days is, at times, too adulatory to ring true
but its obvious bias can be counterbalanced by the savage denunciation in *The Fashionable Tragedian* that followed two years later, edited
and mostly written by William Archer, critic, playwright, and cham-
pion of the new dramas of Bernard Shaw and Ibsen.

Russell reports that Irving based his staging on a new concept of
Hamlet's character:

> 'It is positively laughable to hear Hamlet sneered at for infirmity of
> purpose. . . . Nor is it much less ludicrous to read in an ambitious critique,

that Irving as Hamlet shows an unmanly degree of dejection. As if having to kill your mother's second husband within a few months of your father's murder, upon the injunction of your father's ghost, were a quite ordinary piece of work. . . . The tone and spirit of the whole play, and of Irving's impersonation, and of the Lyceum representation, is at antipodes with such ideas. The mounting of the play has been studiously kept from being too splendid. It is regal, but eminently domestic . . . the apartments of the palace all look habitable. They are not brand new. They are not mere audience chambers. They are usable and used.' (pp. 11–12)

This domestic setting suited Irving's performance, which Russell defined by caustic allusions to earlier actors. His Hamlet:

is no mature dreamer, long accustomed to metaphysical problems, and fond of putting them into fine language [in the Kemble tradition]. . . . Nor is he a mere master of theatrical devices, flooding the stage with tears perhaps at the very moment when Hamlet complains that he cannot weep [in the Edmund Kean tradition]. . . . [In contrast, Irving] has noticed that Hamlet not merely is simple-minded, frankly susceptible, and naturally self-contemplative, but has a trick – not at all uncommon in persons whose most real life is an inner one – *of fostering and aggravating his own excitements.* (pp. 12–13; author's italics)

Irving's Hamlet might be called untheatrical, his frame of mind being set by the situation and imagined in realistic terms in keeping with the 'eminently domestic' stage setting. For example, Russell noted that when Hamlet first met Horatio and said of his 'mother's wedding':

Would I had met my dearest foe in heaven
Or ever I had seen that day, Horatio.

(I.ii.182–3)

Irving discarded the 'bitter, angry, hardhearted way' of other actors. His choice here was to be 'more possessed by his grief at what has happened than by the horrid significance of the image he uses to express it' (pp. 25–6).

The 'most real life' of this Hamlet was an imaginative, inner one, and one that could cause his whole being to be violently excited and

close to hysteria or madness. For example, following the disappearance of the Ghost, Hamlet exclaims, 'O villain, villain, smiling,
damnèd villain!' (I.v.106), and then calls for his 'tablets' so that he can
remember the fact by writing a note about it. The business of
suddenly writing in a notebook is so odd and difficult to act credibly
that many actors avoid the explicit instruction (see Commentary) but
Irving accepted 'the absurdity' as a cue to abandon himself to his
imagination: 'His snatching [the tablets] from his pocket, and writing
on them, is the climax of an outburst hardly distinguishable from
hysteria.' Irving's Hamlet, Russell commented, was like those men
who are 'sane enough in society [but] will pace rooms like wild
animals . . . will talk aloud, will write and tear into fragments many
pages, will do almost anything to find vent for emotions which their
imagination is powerful enough to kindle, but not fertile or methodical enough to satisfy'. However wild Irving became, he kept touch
with ordinary, 'domestic' behaviour whenever possible. His hysteri-
cal reaction to the Ghost slowly subsided and he left the scene 'crav-
ing for human fellowship'; he took his two companions arm by arm
and, with 'bowed head and softened accents', 'said his 'simple last
words, "Let's go together" ' (Russell, pp. 29–33).

Irving emphasized Hamlet's warmth of feeling for others, including Rosencrantz and Guildenstern until they forfeited it, and especially for his father. On first encountering the Ghost with 'I'll call thee
Hamlet, / King, father, royal Dane' (I.iv.44–5), each word was a separate challenge until 'father' provided an emotional and vocal climax;
a pause followed and he 'began a new sentence, "Royal Dane, O,
answer me" ' (Hughes, p. 48). The loss of Ophelia's love drives him
closest to madness. When Ellen Terry joined the cast in 1878, the
intensity of that love made the 'nunnery scene' (III.i.88–150) the
emotional climax of the play. Irving was accused of turning the
tragedy into 'a love poem'. An artist's representation shows Hamlet
and Ophelia standing together with such mutual longing that they
could be mistaken for Romeo and Juliet. Appalled when she gives
back his gifts, he at first takes refuge in a pretended madness but, as
he is racked with pain, physical spasms, and bursts of laughter, the
pretence rapidly becomes a real hysteria. Irving identified 'Ha, ha! Are
you honest?' (l. 103) as the moment when 'the scene takes its sudden

and violent transition'. Other transitions followed: for example, when Hamlet sees Polonius watching and believes that Ophelia has betrayed him, among the brutal words and emotional cruelty, tears could be seen 'welling up' in his eyes as he asks 'Where's your father?' By the side of her grave and moved by the 'bravery' of Laertes' grief, Irving's Hamlet turned for support to Gertrude, 'falling on her neck' as he said 'I loved Ophelia' (Hughes, pp. 56 and 71).

This interpretation of his role guided Irving when he cut and arranged the text. The play had to be made shorter to accommodate the scene changes that showed where each action was happening; the crowds of supernumeraries, needed for the public occasions, took time to come on and off stage; and speech had to be slow if words were to be understood and believable. Much of the cutting was normal practice at the time. Long speeches were abbreviated and offensive and obscure words omitted. Voltemand, Corrnelius, Fortinbras, Reynaldo were excised; Act IV contained little more than Ophelia's madness. On the other hand, a Prompt Book of 1874 shows that the first Court Scene was elaborated by the addition of 13 unnamed Courtiers, five Ladies and, at the back, six 'Men in Chain mail' (Hughes, p. 41, pl. 4). Many small changes and additions served to accentuate Irving's own performance: for example, at the end of the closet scene, Hamlet gave his mother a candle and, with 'good night', sent her to bed; this left Irving alone on stage to speak the scene's last words:

> I must be cruel, only to be kind.
> Thus [*sic*] bad begins, and worse remains behind.

(III.iv.179–80)

Like other actors of the time, he did not say that he would 'lug the guts' of Polonius into another room (l. 213).

Making the play seem to be actually happening was a principal aim behind all Irving's innovations but it was never like ordinary life. It had to be far more controlled and exciting if its increasingly middle-class audiences were to leave their homes to return through the unlit streets of a crowded city. The well appointed Lyceum offered unri-valled and uplifting entertainment in which the performances of

Irving and, later, Ellen Terry were the greatest and unique attractions. He was never less than remarkable, for which William Archer would criticize him as melodramatic and improbable. Other commentators accepted Irving's peculiarities because they compelled attention and accentuated the thrill of revelatory performance:

> In moments of high excitement Irving rapidly plods across and across the stage with a gait peculiar to him – a walk somewhat resembling that of a fretful man trying to get very quickly over a ploughed field. In certain passages his voice has a querulous, piping impatience which cannot be reconciled with stage elegance. . . . [In] his Hamlet there is a strongly marked and courageously preserved individuality, which is more helpful to the due effect of the play than any amount of insipid personal beauty and grace. (Russell, pp. 4–5)

Edward Gordon Craig, actor, visual artist, and play director, who was both his son and biographer, wrote that Irving never walked on the stage but always danced: he 'positively designed . . . dances which fitted perfectly to the speeches given him by Shakespeare' (see Hughes, 1981, p. 14).

John Gielgud

John Gielgud played Hamlet for the first time at the age of twenty-six. As a member of the repertory company at the Old Vic Theatre in London with little time to prepare he was daunted by how much thought and experience was needed, but then, 'suddenly', he said to himself, 'Well, I've just got to be myself' (interview in *Great Acting*, ed. Hal Burton, 1967, p. 140). This performance of 1930 had to draw continually and deeply on his intuition and so did the next in 1934 at the New Theatre in London's West End. This time he also directed the play and so gave himself so much else to do that, close to the opening, he realized that he 'had forgotten [his] own part as an actor' and so, again, his performance had to come alive at each instant as if it were 'improvised' (interview in *The Star*, 16 Nov. 1934). Although some speeches were inaudible on the first night, his performance was praised for its freshness, and during the run he built on that experience. Until he relinquished the role in 1944 at the age of forty, Gielgud's Hamlet was to remain quick thinking, youthful, and recognizably a man of the time.

For the 1934 performance, reviews that appeared the next day differed sharply from those in weekly and monthly publications. The opening had been an euphoric event, partly because Shakespeare was rarely produced in the West End at this time; worthy ventures, like the 1930 transfer of *Hamlet* from the Old Vic to the Queen's Theatre, had had short runs and lost money. The dailies joined in a chorus of almost uniform praise:

> The fire of spirited but introspective youth, and his brilliant scenes of impatience with life, the galling knowledge of his own weakness, and his gentle-mannered light vein with the players and with Polonius carried the house to a climax of a dozen curtain calls.   (*Daily Herald*)

> Here is a production that is beautiful, not spectacular; noble, not pretentious; fresh, not modernistic. That quality of freshness is the most valuable of all . . . an enthusiastic performance of an irresistibly vivid and moving play.   (*Evening News*)

W. A. Darlington of the *Daily Telegraph* gave Gielgud emphatic approval:

> He has youth, he has a romantic presence, he has brains, he has a beautiful voice and the ability to use it beautifully in the speaking of verse. He has the melancholy and the philosophic quality of Hamlet and – most fortunate of all – the ability to suggest the man of action that Hamlet was before the play begins.
>
> In every syllable that he speaks there is evidence of an understanding mind at work, so that the lines come fresh to minds of the audience as if the part has never been acted before.

Some reviewers noted a frame of mind that may now be seen as characteristic of the pre-war 1930s when the more intelligent young spoke of the world with foreboding, in poetry, letters, journalism and everyday talk. In this vein the *Evening Standard* praised a Hamlet 'stung to savage impatience by a herd of mumbling fools who have only wit

enough to turn themselves into a herd of bungling knaves'. In the
Daily Mail, M. Willson Disher sensed that Gielgud's performance had
the same 'vital force' with which he had recently played 'successive
studies of embittered youth' in contemporary plays. The *Daily Express*
was more explicit:

> he cannot forget what century this is. This Hamlet is not 'mad' or 'love-
> sick' – old-fashioned words! He is a witty, sensitive, self-conscious young
> man who knows about complexes and fixations. . . . At last there is a
> good modern play running in town.

Reviewers for the weeklies were noticeably less enthusiastic and
yet had obviously seen the same performance:

> I sat through the tragedy almost unmoved, and quite without excitement.
> . . . [Mr Gielgud's Hamlet] seems aloof and abstracted from everyone and
> everything . . . there is no bitterness in his disdain, no rage in his hatred,
> no affection in his friendship, no wildness in his melancholy.   (*Sunday
> Referee*)

> It was a triumph of expository art. But somehow Hamlet, like ourselves,
> seemed to be outside it all; we [were] interested rather than agonised
> spectators.   (*Observer*)

James Agate in the *Sunday Times* complained that after seeing the
ghost:

> except for one subsequent hurried disarrangement of hair and garments,
> there is never any question, so far as I can detect of the Dane being either
> mad or pretending to be . . . he remains a model of lucidity. . . .
>
>   The scene with the Queen could do with a little less intellectual
> passion and a little more of the other sort. [In Act V, scene ii] his talk of
> ripeness is academic and not the ultimate philosophy of a man who feels
> that his course is run.

Gielgud's Hamlet was reprised in New York during the winter of
1936–7 with a new cast and new scenery and costumes. Of the
production, Rosamond Gilder's *John Gielgud's Hamlet* (1937) provides
an exceptionally detailed and theatrically knowledgeable account. By

this time Gielgud had refined and strengthened his performance. His entrance before 'To be or not to be' was compulsively watchable:

> He comes in, blown on the wind of his excitement. He has been sent for, probably for no good purpose. He looks around, questioning, defiant. Then, seeing no one, drops into his own brooding thoughts. 'To be, or not to be', very quiet, unemphatic; a dark profound, inward note. He walks slowly down the three steps and forward. The lights suspend his thinking face in a timeless abstraction. A deep line cuts the forehead. Each successive idea seems to take form before our eyes as Hamlet pauses, weighs, then moves on to its expression. He makes visible the movement of his mind, so that the concept seems to shine through the transparent mask before the word gives it substance.   (pp. 66–7)

Having played the part for many months, the actor had near-perfect control of speech – for some critics, too noticeably so. When he knelt with outstretched arm before the Ghost:

> Quietly now, the shock relieved by a fronted reality, the deep underlying emotion takes possession of him and moulds the words . . . into pure harmony. The music swells through the sculptured beauty of those magnificent phrases – 'canoniz'd bones', 'hearsed in death', 'quietly inurn'd', 'ponderous and marble jaws' – to a first climax in 'What may this mean?' drops again and reaches a new and different intensity in the 'fools of nature' line with the subsequent anguished 'Wherefore? what should we do?'   (p. 40)

Before the Court entered for the last scene, he paused for a long time, centre-stage, and then:

> He does not move at all, nor is there any rise in inflexion or any marked emphasis on a particular word or phrase, yet each pause marks an increase of power which flows into him and emanates from him as though he were charged with a mysterious invisible current of energy. He seems most poignantly alive as with complete prevision he accepts death. The slow, inward words are an act of renunciation. Very quietly he turns towards Horatio, his hand on his arm. His pale face seems already suspended in eternity. Two words only mark the poignant moment: 'Let be.'   (p. 102)

Gielgud's performance – were it possible to replicate it – would seem too contrived and theatrical today, but in 1936, for Rosamond Gilder, Gielgud had taken Shakespeare's words and 'fill[ed] them to the brim with the life-blood of the "modern man" '. He had grown up in the aftermath of the First World War and knew that 'nobility and brutality were not legends but common facts'. Freudian psychology was widely known and seemed to inform his portrait of a Hamlet who 'is complex, excitable, moody – by turns furious and dejected, violent and indifferent'. He had a 'split personality', a 'mother-fixation', and a 'sense of guilt' (p. 7). This Hamlet 'is not mad . . . [but] occasionally dominated by a force within himself that he cannot master. . . . [His] problem, as Gielgud presents it, is not a matter of lack of will, courage, or determination . . . but of an unresolved discord within himself' (p. 9).

In presenting this 'modern man', the actor had such a complete mastery of his craft that Hamlet:

> seems born again every night. He hears what is said to him as if for the first time, feels freshly his grief and bitter disgust. . . . Though absorbed by his inner conflict, he reacts instantaneously to every impact from the unsympathetic world around him. This aliveness is expressed in every fibre of Gielgud's performance and is part of its dominant quality of young sensitiveness. For his Hamlet is the revolt of youth at the destruction of its faith in truth and decency and love.   (pp. 11–12)

Jo Mielziner's stage setting for New York was splendid and stately in effect but its form was simple, in a manner that looked back to Gordon Craig's designs earlier in the century. It satisfied Gielgud's professed need for 'the sense of pictorial richness and sensuous decadence of a Renaissance court' (Gilder, p. 117), as had Motley's design for the London production in 1934. Both settings also avoided lengthy scene changes which would have severely hampered Gielgud's careful management of climaxes and silences. For one reviewer the London production had been 'a triumph in its simplicity, swiftness, and sense of sombre colour, with the notes of silver and of bronze in the curtains and the fascinating Jacobean costumes of "Motley's" designing' (*Morning Post*). The innovatory way in which times past had been evoked was in accord with the modernity of Gielgud's interpretation of a Renaissance prince.

He performed the role and directed the play again in 1939 and 1944, after which he decided that he was too old to play the 'young Hamlet' but he continued to pay fastidious attention to the text and would talk and, occasionally, write about the demands it makes on present-day actors and directors. In the summer of 1963 he felt able to accept an invitation to direct the play once more, with Richard Burton as Hamlet in a production to be part of New York's celebration of Shakespeare's 400th birthday. Richard L. Sterne's *John Gielgud Directs Richard Burton in Hamlet* (1967) gives a close-up view of the rehearsals and early performances. Its author was an actor who played a 'Gentleman' and 'Player Musician' and to whom Gielgud had given permission to eavesdrop on all rehearsals and keep a journal. By this means, Sterne's book reports verbatim many of Gielgud's comments on the text and performance, as the production developed.

Gielgud had had second thoughts on staging and costuming. There would be no imitation of a Renaissance world because, he said, the arrival of scenery and lighting can 'cramp the imagination'. Instead the set would be bare boards (but on several levels) and the play would be performed 'as if in its final run-through, before the technical rehearsals begin'. (Perhaps he was thinking of the unfinished conditions in which he had given his first performances in 1930 and 1934.) The actors wore 'rehearsal clothes', chosen to suit each individual in the play and changing with the time of day and situation (Sterne, pp. 12–13). During rehearsals, he would sometimes remind the actors of Elizabethan concern with rank and decorum but he also asked them to reflect contemporary life: Polonius and Gertrude were to be 'great cronies who probably play bridge together on Saturday' (p. 35). He cut the flourish of trumpets in the first Court scene, replacing it with 'loud' improvised talking that yields to a sudden 'hush' on the king's approach (pp. 25–6). Although the setting and some of the action looked improvised, Gielgud wanted the actors to retain the subtlety and complexity of Shakespeare's verse. Sterne records him telling Richard Burton: 'Your line "weary, stale, flat and unprofitable" – I think you've got to find each of those words out of the other. You can't take them all as one phrase. Think of each word before you say it' (p. 78). He rewarded a less experienced actor

with: 'Beautiful, your performance, Marcellus, beautiful – very sensitive and lovely' (p. 87). He wanted the production to have it both
ways, to be recognizably of the moment and extraordinarily rich and
complex in speech and thought processes.

In Sterne's account, Gielgud was more concerned about the stage
and Shakespeare's words than about the world outside the theatre.
For him, the play expressed the thoughts and feelings of individuals.
As a director he sought 'successive climaxes. . . . The driving force of
[Hamlet's] emotion, his power to imagine . . . the onrush . . . the
upward sweep . . . the downward drop', rather than clarification of
narrative or theme (see Gilder, pp. 8–9). He developed visual and
aural impressions rather than clarifying the play's narrative and
theme or depicting social and political realities. Those matters would
be the concern of later directors and actors.

Peter Hall and David Warner

Memory can still recall images from Peter Hall's production for the
Royal Shakespeare Company at Stratford-upon-Avon in 1965 and
the impression it made on its audiences. The first night performance
gave no clear indication of the landmark status it would achieve. At
its end many audience members stayed sitting on their hands and
few reviewers for the dailies could think what the director and his
twenty-four-year-old prince, David Warner, were about. Where was
the excitement, the deep feeling, or the 'poetry'? Much of the text had
been spoken slowly and the performance lasted four and quarter
hours. At the dramatic climax of the 'play scene' (Act III, scene ii),
Claudius left the stage calling for lights in a subdued voice. Those still
watching noted that Hamlet smiled as he killed the king and was
quietly laughing as he himself died: what could he be thinking?
Reviewers for the Sunday papers, with more time for reflection,
recognized that a constant re-thinking of the text marked this
production apart from others. The director had reasoned out his
approach and wanted his audience to follow him by using their
minds.

Much of this might have been expected since Peter Hall had

recently completed a cycle of history plays that also brought revaluations. Those concerning Henry VI, among the earliest of Shakespeare's texts, were reduced from three plays to two but staged so that their conflicts and contrasts always made political sense. The better known *Henry IV* and *Henry V* were no longer colourful pageants but presented in a way that magnified their violence and cruelty while clarifying self-interest and political double-talk. The same qualities and many of the same actors were in Hall's production of *Hamlet* but here, on the first night, many critics found them unacceptable: this play should be a tragedy, and its emotion, mystery and philosophical depth respected.

The director made no secret of his intentions but had published the talk he gave to the actors at the start of rehearsals. He had sought a meaning geared to his view of the present:

> There is a sense of what-the-hell-anyway; over us looms the mushroom cloud [of an atom bomb]. And politics are a game and a lie, whether in our own country or in the East–West dialogue, which goes on interminably without anything very real being said. The middle-aged have betrayed us. Or so the young think.

Peter Hall was thirty-five years old, David Warner twenty-four. For them Hamlet:

> has been trapped into a compulsory situation he does not want but which has been forced upon him. . . . A man is crucified by an experience so complex that it leads to a profound disillusionment and finally a terrible fatalism. (*Observer*, 15 August 1965)

This advance publicity might have been one reason why the *Stratford-upon-Avon Herald* reported all-night queues of young people, some of them having already seen a preview. The 'overwhelming cheers' of this part of the audience, sitting or standing at the back, had greeted the end of the performance while response elsewhere was perfunctory.

For many years now, directors of Shakespeare have been re-interpreting the plays by emphasizing their relevance to the present time, contemporary 'versions' and modern-dress productions being rarities no longer. But in Peter Hall's 1965 production a pursuit of relevance had led to the scrutiny of every word in the long text and a determination to speak them meaningfully and, wherever possible, in ways that were immediately recognizable to its audiences. The gain in intelligibility was judged to be worth the performance lasting longer than usual.

As the production settled into the repertoire, audiences got its measure more readily and would perceptibly respond with mental recognitions. For some reviewers this effect had been present on the opening night. Unremarkable words were spoken as if each one had to be weighed: 'I . . . do . . . not . . . know . . . why . . . yet . . . I . . . live. . . .' When Polonius interrupts the Player's Aeneas speech, the inflection of Hamlet's 'Come to Hecuba' expressed his weariness at the interference and was reinforced with a gesture 'almost comically helpless and weary'. When armed men enter to bring him before the King, 'Here they come' was spoken with a colloquial emphasis on *they* that expressed his loathing of a restrictive and uncomprehending authority; the one word was no longer the simple identification it seems to be on a printed page. For the anonymous critic of *The Times*, Hamlet's soliloquies were 'an almost pedantically articulate attempt to impose a meaning on his inner chaos'. For Ronald Bryden of the *New Statesman* they were:

> the greatest triumph of the production: using the Elizabethan convention with total literalness, Hamlet communicates not with himself but with you. For the first time in my experience, the rhetoric, spoken as it was intended to be, comes brilliantly to life.

The casting of David Warner perfectly matched Peter Hall's purposes. He came to the role with few preconceptions but with the experience of joining the Royal Shakespeare Company straight from drama school and in four years progressing rapidly through Lysander in the *Dream*, to Henry the Sixth and Richard the Second, and on to the innocent fool, Valentine Brose, in Henry Livings's contemporary comedy, *Eh?* As Hamlet, he was entirely at ease with his director's lead and played with a rare nakedness, seldom seeming to strive for effect. His voice was sometimes soft, sometimes raw, and seldom elegant. His long arms flailed in emphasis or impatience.

With designer John Bury, Peter Hall presented a suitable world for this prince. Spaces were large with fixtures of black wood and floors that shone like marble. Clothes were sober and in heavy materials, late Renaissance in silhouette rather than in detail. Stage properties and stage business belonged more to bureaucracy and politics than to Renaissance courts and private life; for example, in Act I, scene ii:

> Claudius' first meeting with the Privy Council, with Hamlet imprisoned at the table was far more telling than the ostentatious solitude in which he is usually set apart. That table was the cage of circumstance in which he was caught up. (*Shakespeare Quarterly*, 1965)

Behaviour was often unaffected and matter-of-fact. Hamlet wore and handled a long red scarf in what was then a familiar student fashion. Polonius took a drink at times of reflection and passed official papers to his king as if he were a high-ranking civil servant 'in a meeting' with his prime minister. When Gertrude met with her son in the bedroom, her wig had come off. Groups of officials moved discreetly and predictably. All this familiarized the play's action and invited the audience to see Shakespeare's play in a meaningful context.

Overall the direction seemed soft, appearing never to hurry the actors, and yet it was endlessly busy with new readings of the text and with manifestations of life at the present time. The production did not grab attention but securely held it once spectators allowed that to happen. In more recent years many other productions have given a similar up-to-date gloss to Shakespeare but this one had the shock of all truly original art by relying more than most on an intelligent 'reading' of the dialogue: this director seemed to have rehearsed with a copy of the text in his hand. And more than many other directors of the time, Peter Hall had been aware of the need to sell his political and contemporary credentials. He had publicly declared his determination that the RSC should be a theatre company 'expert in the past but alive to the present' (*Stratford Herald* 4 March 1966).

Hamlet in many forms

During the last decades of the twentieth century and at the beginning of the twenty-first, productions of *Hamlet* became so numerous and, in method and effect, so varied that no one book, however large, could do justice to all the most notable of them. How best to perform Shakespeare has never been so open to question: in this electronic age, staging has become more efficient and fluid, marketing more competitive, and the acting profession financially dominated by film and television. Power now rests with producers and institutions, hardly ever with individual actors and only occasionally with directors. Audiences often find that going to the theatre is difficult as well as expensive. Performance standards are unpredictable and all but a few productions lack sufficient funding. The only undoubted advantage of technology is that, even when alone and at home, most of us can view Shakespeare's most popular plays in film versions or TV recordings. In these circumstances, the recent life of *Hamlet* in the theatre is represented here by a selective roll-call of very different productions, with brief indications of what was on offer.

Buzz Goodbody's 1975 production at Stratford-upon-Avon attracted immediate attention. Staged in an adapted costume store with a small but experienced cast, an audience of a few hundred seated close to the stage, and a recent university graduate as director (and also the first woman to direct for the RSC), the play made a more direct and intense appeal than the company's elaborate productions on its main stage. The Hamlet of Ben Kingsley seemed entirely open to the audience, both physical and mental responses evident to all. A vogue for small-scale productions was to follow, especially among companies with minimal resources. As one example among countless others, Sam Walters's 1985 production at the Orange Tree in Richmond, London, made its distinctive mark by using the First Quarto text, and was played in the round with only a couple of hundred spectators. *City Limits* hailed its 'compelling narrative' and a performance that was 'heady and dangerous'. B. A. Young in the *Financial Times* declared that he would 'never again think of a "bad quarto" as being a bad play. As we have it here it is thrilling.'

In larger scale also, the familiar text has often been unexpectedly changed in pursuit of new readings and new looks for the play. At London's Royal Court Theatre in 1980, the whole of the first scene was cut and there was no Ghost to visit Jonathan Pryce's Hamlet; instead he was possessed by his dead father, whose words were retched up from deep within his body. Richard Eyre's production tried consistently to be believable: the Court of Elsinore was a close-knit group, a politically minded, mutually suspicious, and well established hierarchy among whom Hamlet was an instinctive loner, acerbic and dissatisfied rather than philosophical and incapable of action. The setting by Antony McDonald for Ron Daniel's production at Stratford in 1989 was unexpected:

> the whole world is, literally, out of joint. Elsinore is seen as an imprisoning institution where the side-walls incline inwards, where the cornices run at odd angles to the floor and where a huge, Magritte-like rear window gives on to a swirling spindrift.   (*Guardian*)

Mark Rylance as Hamlet veered 'between tremulous weakness and mad pranks' (*Sunday Telegraph*), his real and pretended madness 'somehow seamlessly consistent with an ineffable and injured spirituality' (*Independent*). Another reviewer reported that 'layer upon layer of mental disturbance is uncovered as he sidles towards a violent escape from a world he cannot bear' (*Daily Mail*).

The press has not always been sympathetic towards textual liberties or directorial inventions. Back in 1974, when a more reverent attitude was expected, the *Spectator* was scathing about an experienced and widely admired director:

> Belting through the piece in less than three hours, trimming out characters and scenes with larkish abandon, he has unfleshed a masterpiece to reveal a skeletal melodrama with no intellectual sinew and little dramatic muscle.

When *Hamlet* is performed in translation a measure of freedom is inevitable and major changes to the play have become commonplace. Since everyday speech can be used instead of words written centuries ago, unmistakable references to current concerns and celebrities are used to accentuate the play's contemporary relevance. In Yuri Lyubimov's production at the Taganka Theatre, Moscow, in 1971, Vladimir Vysotsky, a popular protest-poet and singer, played Hamlet without hiding his own personality or role in society. An open grave and the gravediggers were on stage at the start of the performance and then Hamlet entered alone and performed Pasternak's banned 'Hamlet' poem, accompanying himself on his guitar (see Spenser Golub, *Foreign Shakespeare*, ed. D. Kennedy, Cambridge, 1993, pp. 158–77).

Ingmar Bergman's 1986–7 Stockholm production was set in the present and recent past and made allusions to two World Wars. Peter Stormare's Hamlet was driven by pain, violent fury and despair, rather than by duty, uncertainty or idealism. 'To be or not to be' was transposed so that it was spoken to the Players, the only persons who might understand him. At the end, Fortinbras and his terrorist-revolutionaries break down the high wall that backed the acting area, Horatio is shot, and the closing words of Fortinbras are spoken after Hamlet's corpse has been put on public display (see L.-L. and F. J. Marker, *Ingmar Bergman*, Cambridge, 1992, pp. 261–71).

Peter Hall, at the National Theatre in 1976, was among the directors in Britain and North America who continued to use period dress and as much as practicable of a text drawn from both the Second Quarto and the Folio. Sometimes such conservatism has gone along with up-dated staging as in Laurence Boswell's 1999 production at the Young Vic, which placed the audience on two sides of a long platform. The director's innovations included a Ghost walking on stilts, and Hamlet dressing up in a wig and crown of thorns to taunt Claudius, and washing Yorick's skull while taking a bath. The use of a full text went along with care for how it was spoken: the *Sunday Telegraph* commented that, far from undergoing a 'spirit-lowering ordeal', one came away after four hours 'feeling that this really is the only way the play should be done'. Of Paul Rhys's Hamlet, reviews were almost unanimous:

> The performance pulsates with intelligence and feeling . . . I would not have missed it for anything.   (*Sunday Times*)

> Rhys is a revelation. Whether being a weeping student . . . or a frantic psychotic, he keeps his lean face open but watchful. . . . As a result, his madness is unaffectedly credible.   (*Independent on Sunday*)

> In Paul Rhys . . . Boswell has found an actor capable of getting an audience to hang upon the tortured Dane's every utterance.   (*Time Out*)

Other reviews registered reservations: 'In Rhys's detailed, beautifully spoken if slightly precious performance, all that's missing is the sexiness' (*Mail on Sunday*).

For a production at New York's Public Theater in 1990, Kevin Kline both played the lead and directed the play – as Gielgud and Irving had done before him – and used an almost full text. In *Village Voice*, this theatrical conservatism – and courage – won Michael Feingold's approval:

> His minimal, carefully low-key production strips the play bare and lays it out clean to the spectator's eye. . . . In three decades of hearing *Hamlets*, British and American, I can't remember one so lucidly spoken, in which nearly every phrase communicates not only its sense but its emotional weight.

But not everyone agreed; for example, Frank Rich of the *New York Times*:

> If Mr Kline has something pressing to say about this character . . . it is not articulated. The man behind Hamlet's various poses remains the wrong sort of mystery throughout, a remote blank rather than a compelling enigma.

Having played Hamlet four years earlier in a production by Liviu Ciulei, Kline was asked in an interview why this time he chose to direct himself: his reply was that 'he wanted his Hamlet to be his own and not someone else's'. The desire is simple and understandable but its accomplishment within limited time, in a technically well-equipped theatre and with a cast drawn from many sources, is almost certainly impossible, except for very well disposed audiences.

In theatre at the start of the present century, the interest that was once focused on *Hamlet*'s title role has widened to encompass the world in which the action takes place and its reflection of current political and social issues. As part of this change, many adaptations have been produced that make their own statements by means of various degrees of dependence on Shakespeare's text. The plays considered in Ruby Cohn's *Modern Shakespeare Off-shoots* (1976) date from 1948 onwards and extend from complete re-writing to textual rearrangement and burlesque. Action has frequently been re-located in time and place or given a different ending: sometimes, almost nothing of Shakespeare's dialogue remains. Tom Stoppard's *Rosencrantz and Guildenstern are Dead* (1966), which has proved to be one of the few durable theatrical 'offshoots', relegates a performance of Shakespeare's text to an occasional part of another play that involves Shakespeare's characters in games, jokes, boredom, and uncertainty that are indebted to Samuel Beckett's *Waiting for Godot*, which had had its first performance in English in 1955.

Heiner Müller's *The Hamlet Machine* was published in 1977 but, immediately facing East German censorship, not performed until 1979 in Paris in a French translation. Occupying only a few pages in print and, unlike ordinary dramatic texts, leaving much to director, designer and actors in making a performance, what remains of *Hamlet* is part of a site on which to erect an image of political oppression and intellectual self-examination in the context of European history. Ophelia concludes the play by 'Fiercely Enduring Millennia': according to the text, she sits in a wheelchair, motionless and wrapped in white gauze, while '*Fish, debris, dead bodies and limbs drift by.*' Andy Lavender's *Hamlet in Pieces: Shakespeare Reworked* (2001) does not consider play texts but original stage productions that have been derived from Shakespeare's text by three theatre directors, Peter Brook, Robert Lepage, and Robert Wilson, each reforming and reworking the play to suit their own, contemporary vision. Time may well show that the key performances and productions of *Hamlet* will in future be found not in established theatres and companies but wherever theatrical innovation is strongest or, alternatively, in the very different media of film and television.

5 *The Play on Screen*

Directors using the lens media learned to make good use of Shakespeare's texts in films that have many echoes of theatrical space and performance. Their work has won a far wider audience than the most admired theatre productions. Although *Hamlet* is far more reliant on a brilliant use of words than any film script, its fast-moving and varied action has proved particularly well suited to a cinema screen. Inevitably, the dominance of visual images in a film has changed an audience's experience but some qualities of the text are revealed that might well be missed by a reader or theatre audience. The play's characters can be shown in close-up or given greater scope for movement and change in a wide filmic setting. While the dialogue will always be cut more or less drastically, the director's handling of time and focus can heighten the impact of a few chosen words, which will be under greater control than in a theatre and from which an audience's attention is less able to stray.

As a means of learning more about Shakespeare's text, a film of *Hamlet* is no adequate substitute for a theatre performance or an imaginative reading, but some films can make us more aware of the play's social and cultural context and its place in history. For moments at least, the unspoken responses of the play's characters will be more evident and give prominence to their physical and sensual involvement with each other. Seeing a number of films will demonstrate how differently Shakespeare's text can be interpreted, and develop a critical response to performance and production.

Before making his 1964 film of *Hamlet*, Grigori Kozintsev knew the text very well, having directed the play at the Pushkin Theatre in Leningrad in 1953. Filmed in black and white for cinemascope, the world presented on screen is a vast fortified palace in bleak surroundings, an isolated and sumptuous stronghold built on rock at the shore of a restless sea. Shakespeare could never have visited such a place but, in the film, it serves as a constant reminder of 'the prison' that Elsinore is for Hamlet (II.ii.243–50). Innokenti Smoktunovsky is a physically strong and intellectually careful prince, very different from the temperamental hero of most British theatre productions, who at times is close to madness. This Hamlet is often slow and habitually serious in speech, adopting tempos and rhythms that would be difficult if the text were spoken in English and projected for a large audience. Yet at times the words reproduced in the film's subtitles ring true and become a reminder of the weight of responsibility and depth of feeling that belong to the Hamlet of Shakespeare's text – a reminder, too, that Elizabeth's England was a police state with centralized power, in which spying and betrayal were everyday events – not so very unlike Soviet Russia at the time this film was made. In these respects Kozintsev's film leads us towards a fuller response to the play.

The short script for the film, lasting 142 minutes, made large cuts in the play text, often reducing soliloquies and the longer speeches to a few lines. Almost always it was spoken slowly: for Kozintsev's purposes, the 'English method' of reading the full text in a rapid rhythm leads to a blunting of perception. In this flow of verse, the thoughts and images are not grasped, do not 'penetrate' (Kozintsev, 1996, p. 274). Adding to the chosen 'seriousness' of the film – it has very few laughs – the play's action has been supplemented with silent episodes: relentless waves of the sea, horses being ridden, neighing, and about to break free; the Court engaged in 'heavy-headed revel' (I.iv.17) while Hamlet is about to meet his father's Ghost; Ophelia reading Hamlet's poem, being instructed in a slow dance, and submitting as she is buckled into an inflexible corset and dressed in black for her father's funeral; Hamlet on board ship dealing with the sleeping Rosencrantz and Guildenstern. Fortinbras and his army become more prominent than in the play as they approach and take over Elsinore: Kozintsev's journal explains what he sought:

> With a heavy tread, covered with dust, long unshaven, wearing dirt-stained boots and heavy armor, the men of fire and iron march. They go to act. The man of heart and thought is dead. (p. 270)

For some of the splendid trappings of power, this Russian film borrowed from one made earlier by Laurence Olivier with himself as Hamlet and a cast mostly of experienced theatre actors. His flawlessly phrased soliloquies spoken as voice-overs might well have influenced Kozintsev's use of the same device but, where Olivier's Hamlet sits alone at a distance from the Court, Smoktunovsky's Russian Hamlet keeps moving silently among courtiers who are busy with their own affairs. Olivier's soliloquies provide the most directly affecting parts of a film that now seems almost ludicrously theatrical, despite numerous long shots, changes of focus, and silent picturesque passages that include Ophelia floating dead in a flower-decked stream. Its frequently ringing tones of voice appear unreal and simplistic today and so does an opening statement that pronounces 'This is the tragedy of a man who could not make up his mind.'

Tony Richardson's film of 1969 with Nicol Williamson as Hamlet was shot within the bare brick walls of the Roundhouse in London where the same cast and director had recently staged the play. The contrast with Olivier and Kozintsev could hardly be greater. Uninterested in splendour and using minimal visual resources and many long takes, Richardson relied on unaffected acting and the interplay of persons completely caught up in their own needs and desires and in what the words mean to them. For viewers wanting a film coming as close to a theatre performance as cameras are able, this might be the best choice, despite its visual and spatial restrictions.

In a far fuller filmic manner, with long vistas and carefully observed details, Franco Zeffirelli's *Hamlet* of 1990 has other, less obtrusive theatrical qualities. No stage production preceded the making of this film but its director's experience of staging Shakespeare (including *Romeo and Juliet* and *Much Ado About Nothing* in London) has influenced his handling of the text and his well-chosen actors. Performances are fluent and subtle, Shakespeare's words seeming to present no difficulty but enhancing an impression of quick-changing sensations and very precise thinking. With the camera holding a steady focus on him, Mel Gibson's Hamlet was able to speak the soliloquies slowly and thoughtfully. Yet Zeffirelli was not overly restrained by the film script's theatrical origin, cutting or transposing many of its lines and adding new silent episodes. His determination to make everything visually clear to an audience is announced at the very start of the film, which is not on the battlements and requires no ghostly presence: in place of that, Gertrude is seen grieving over her dead husband – 'like Niobe, all tears' is the play's description of this (I.ii.149) – as Hamlet casts earth into his father's grave. The film then moves to the play's second scene, set in a stone hall and presented with much panoply and public gravity, in contrast with which Glenn Close's Gertrude laughs at the wordplay of her son's 'I am too much in the sun' and Gibson's Hamlet takes 'Ay, madam, it is common' very slowly and hesitates an appreciable time before saying 'I shall in all my best obey you, madam.'

The words of the script are old, as are the actors' costumes and courtly behaviour, but the performances, at their best, are instinctively alive in the present moment. The camera often directs attention to Gertrude, so that her part in the story can seldom be forgotten: for example, she is seen to be dumbstruck as she watches Hamlet's elation after *The Mousetrap* has exposed Claudius's guilt. The few words she speaks convey deep-seated feelings and, as the film draws to its close, great strength of mind. Held on camera during her wide-eyed madness, Helena Bonham-Carter's Ophelia is mentally in pain and physically unapproachable and dangerous: the intensity of her suffering commands both the pity and wonder of audiences. At moments like these, the camera is more coldly observant than a theatre audience could ever be and Zeffirelli has made space and given time in which to draw attention to an astonishing performance from an actress very used to the camera's scrutiny. Here the film's sustained focus on the performer's physical presence is offset and enhanced by a wider view and clearly spoken words.

Kenneth Branagh's film features himself as Hamlet, a role he had previously acted in a theatre production. The show-business gloss of its Edwardian dress and an energy and clarity in speech render it old-fashioned in comparison with Zeffirelli's more filmic version. To a lesser and greater degree both these films seem confined by the theatrical origin of their scripts and by residual mannerisms of theatre production, qualities that are still more evident when viewed alongside Michael Almereyda's *Hamlet* made at the turn of the century. This film hauls Shakespeare's play into the present time by setting its action in the high-tech business world of today's Manhattan. The kingdom of Denmark becomes the Denmark Corporation, an organization that exercises global power with ruthless efficiency. Its prince is alienated from this executive world and also an amateur film-maker whose *Mousetrap* is screened in Claudius's private cinema. In this process, Shakespeare's text is left far behind and often drops out of view entirely – although not for those who know its words well. Such will always tend to be the case when a play is successfully transferred from theatre to another medium that has its own distinctive language, whether that is film, classical ballet, modern dance, opera, or novel.

A reader of Shakespeare's *Hamlet* who has no opportunity of seeing a theatre production or rehearsal will gain a better understanding of the performative nature of its text by viewing a number of these films, one after another, choosing those that use film in different ways and, if possible, not omitting an earlier one that is close to theatre in speech and physical enactment. At the same time, the context of the play's action and the many different ways in which its words can work for an audience will unavoidably register in the viewer's mind. If only one film can be viewed, the best choice would be Zeffirelli's version, which retains and significantly develops some of the means proper to theatre.

6 Critical Assessments

Ever since the early days of the play's life, long before criticism became an established discourse, *Hamlet* has aroused curiosity and controversy. In 1661, John Evelyn ranked *Hamlet* among 'the old plays [that] begin to disgust this refined age' (*Diary*, 26 November) and yet its popular theatrical success remained beyond all doubt. For the aspiring dramatist George Farquhar (1667–1707), it had long been 'the darling of the English Audience, and like to continue with the same applause, in defiance of all the criticism that were ever publish'd in Greek, and Latin' (*Discourse upon Comedy*, 1702). As a tragedy, however, it was to remain morally and psychologically puzzling: its hero was not exemplary, its action neither regular nor inevitable. In his edition of 1765, Samuel Johnson identified 'variety' as the play's distinguishing excellence but objected that some scenes 'neither forward nor retard' the action and that Hamlet is 'rather an instrument than an agent':

> After he has, by the stratagem of the play, convicted the King, he makes no attempt to punish him, and his death is at last effected by an incident which Hamlet has no part in producing. The catastrophe is not very happily produced; the exchange of weapons is rather an expedient of necessity, than a stroke of art. The poet is accused of having shown little regard to poetical justice, and may be charged with equal neglect of poetical probability.

Nevertheless, Hamlet's fame as a character spread widely and his moral qualities were frequently debated. To the titular hero of Goethe's *Wilhelm Meister's Apprenticeship* (1795–6):

> A lovely, pure, noble and most moral nature, without the strength of nerve which forms a hero, sinks beneath a burden which it cannot bear and must

not cast away. Impossibilities have been required of him; not in themselves impossibilities, but such for him. He winds, and turns, and torments
himself; he advances and recoils ... at last [he] does all but lose his
purpose from his thoughts, yet still without recovering his peace of mind.

To readers in tune with the English romantic poets, Hamlet could
seem eminently understandable and not unlike themselves. Samuel
Coleridge (1772–1834), poet and critic, judged him as he judged
himself:

Hamlet's character is the prevalence of the abstracting and generalizing
habit over the practical. He does not want courage, skill, will, or opportunity; but every incident sets him thinking; and it is curious, and at the
same time strictly natural, that Hamlet, who all the play seems reason
itself, should be impelled, at last, by mere accident to effect his object. I
have a smack of Hamlet myself, if I may say so.   (*Table Talk*, 1827)

William Hazlitt (1778–1830) declared Hamlet's speeches and sayings
were 'as real as our own thoughts. Their reality is in the reader's mind.
It is *we* who are Hamlet.' In the theatre this critic blamed any short-
coming on the actors, finding fault with both Kemble and Kean (see
p. 135, above), as if the character itself were beyond any censure:

Mr Kemble plays it like a man in armour, with a determined inveteracy of
purpose, in one undeviating straight line, which is as remote from the
natural grace and refined susceptibility of the character, as the sharp
angles and abrupt starts which Mr Kean introduces into the part. ...
There should be as much of the gentleman and scholar as possible
infused into the part, and as little of the actor.   (*Characters of Shakespeare's
Plays*, 1817)

By the end of the nineteenth century, the play had been accepted
as both masterpiece and challenge. Edward Dowden's *Shakespere: A
Critical Study of his Mind and Art* (1875) set a tone of high seriousness
and bafflement:

Shakspere had left far behind him that early stage of development when
an artist obtrudes his intentions, or distrusting his own ability to keep
sight of one uniform design, deliberately and with effort holds that design

persistently before him. When Shakspere completed *Hamlet* he must have trusted himself and trusted his audience; he trusts himself to enter into relation with his subject, highly complex as that subject was, in a pure, emotional manner. *Hamlet* might so easily have been manufactured into an enigma, or a puzzle; and then the puzzle, if sufficient pains were bestowed, could be completely taken to pieces and explained. But Shakspere created it a mystery, and therefore it is forever suggestive . . . and never wholly explicable.

Among those who took up the challenge, A. C. Bradley was the most rigorous. His grasp of detail and sensitivity to words gave to his *Shakespearean Tragedy* (1904) an authority that still wins respect today. Like many critics before him, he was concerned with the 'character' of Hamlet but he did not judge him by words or deeds alone. For example, of his humour, he says, 'those of his retorts which strike one as perfectly individual do so, I think, chiefly because they suddenly reveal the misery and bitterness below the surface'. As instances he quoted: 'We shall obey, were she ten times our mother' (III.ii.340) and, in answer to 'Will you walk out of the air, my lord?', 'Into my grave?' (II.ii.206–8) – words that 'suddenly turn one cold' (p. 122). Bradley also insisted that attention should *not* concentrate solely on Hamlet (see p. 139) and, in consequence, argued that his meeting with a pirate ship on his journey to England (see IV.vi.15–21) was not a 'lame expedient' of plotting, as many had said, but the first of a number of 'accidents' in which, as Hamlet says, 'heaven [is] ordinant' (V.ii.48, and see ll. 10–11). As the final stages of the action unfold, these happenings:

> strengthen in the spectator the feeling that, whatever may become of Hamlet, and whether he wills it or not, his task will surely be accomplished, because it is the purpose of a power against which both he and his enemy are impotent, and which makes of them the instruments of its own will. . . . The apparent failure of Hamlet's life is not the ultimate truth concerning him.   (pp. 140–1)

With Bradley, critical argument about *Hamlet* came of age and has continued in vigorous health to the present day. Several main lines can be distinguished.

(i)   Verbal style

In tune with Bradley's subtle investigations and with an increased awareness of the subconscious, close attention to verbal images brought a new understanding of the structure of the play. Caroline Spurgeon's *Shakespeare's Imagery and What it Tells Us* (1935) was an early study of this kind. She argued that, to Shakespeare's pictorial imagination, 'the problem in *Hamlet* is not predominantly that of will and reason'. Judging by the images in the text, she no longer saw its subject as:

> the problem of an individual at all, but as something greater and even more mysterious, as a *condition* for which the individual himself is apparently not responsible, any more than the sick man is to blame for the infection which strikes and devours him, but which, nevertheless, in its course and development, impartially and relentlessly, annihilates him and others, innocent and guilty alike. That is the tragedy of *Hamlet*, as it is perhaps the chief tragic mystery of life.   (pp. 318–19)

Many critics adopted a similar position and viewed the play as a poem in which verbal images carried 'hidden' meanings. Early examples are G. Wilson Knight's *The Shakespearian Tempest* (1932) and D. A. Stauffer, *Shakespeare's World of Images: The Development of his Moral Ideas* (1969). Others used the same means, together with attention to irregular syntax, metrical or rhythmic emphasis, strange or unexpected choice of words, sudden transitions of sentiment or subject, and all sorts of verbal nicety and 'speech actions', and in this way revealed subtextual changes in thought and feeling that exist beneath the primary meanings of spoken words. Examples are M. M. Mahood, *Shakespeare's Wordplay* (1957) and Norman Rabkin, *Shakespeare and the Problem of Meaning* (1981). Having attended to 'revealing tones and implications' in Shakespeare's choice of words, L. C. Knights found a complex play of attitudes, and *Hamlet* became a study 'of the mind's engagement with the world, of the intimate and intricate relations of self and world' (*'Hamlet' and other Shakespearean Essays*, 1979, pp. 191 and 80). This new criticism tended to turn Shakespeare into a dramatist concerned with intellectual 'problems' and 'the question of moral judgement'.

   Detailed textual exegesis also became an accepted part of the
study of the play in performance, the interests of critics and actors
interacting and becoming closer. Michael Goldman's *Acting and
Action in Shakespearean Tragedy* (1985) is concerned with rhetorical
structure and the demands that the text makes on the physical
performance of actors. Marvin Rosenberg and Robert Hapgood have
collected evidence about how actors of many kinds have used the
words of the text (*The Masks of Hamlet*, 1992, and *Hamlet in Performance*,
1999). The Commentary of this Handbook links close textual enquiry
to a study of the play's enactment on stage and an audience's experience of performance (see, for example, the notes on I.ii.176–89;
I.v.112–20; II.i.1–26; III.i.93–162; III.iv.171–80).

(ii)   *Action and plot*

Criticism became concerned with what the play *does*, not only with
what it *says*. In *The Unnatural Scene: A Study in Shakespearean Tragedy*
(1976), Michael Long argued that the text 'constantly has the means to
create and reveal new facets of the dynamic presentation of
[Hamlet's] mind in its social world which escape any easily reductive
categorization' (p. 148). Published in the same year, Ernst
Honigmann's *Seven Tragedies Revisited: The Dramatist's Manipulation of
Response* is acutely aware of the audience's changing perceptions or,
in L. C. Knights's phrase, its 'moral judgement':

> Like Hamlet, we tend to believe in the Ghost when we see it, and to
> distrust it when we have time to reflect; like Hamlet again, we first believe
> in the rightness of revenge, then, prompted by the play, we grow uneasy
> about it.   (p. 76)

Beneath these ever-changing intellectual impressions, the story
can seem to grow to 'something of great constancy' (*A Midsummer
Night's Dream*, V.i.26) and that, too, has increasingly engaged the
attention of critics. Harley Granville Barker, actor, playwrigh, and
director, set a clear example in his *Preface* to *Hamlet* (1937) by studying
the play 'for its action as a thing of movement' (p. vi). Paradoxically,
he concluded that Shakespeare had not 'finally *dramatised* Hamlet' (p.

13; his italics): – he had tried to 'reconcile the creature of his imagination with the figure of the borrowed story [his lost source]; the
Hamlet we have is the tragic product of his very failure to do so' (p.
290). From the start, in Barker's view, Hamlet is inwardly divided,
weakened, and 'at odds with himself': and this 'unbalance' or discor-
dance is the primary effect of the play in performance:

> While our age of doubt endures, and men still cry despairingly 'I do not
> know . . .' [IV.iv.43] and must go uncomforted, the play will keep, I
> should suppose, its hold on us.   (p. 329)

In a frequently republished and quoted essay of 1960 on 'The
Jacobean Shakespeare', Maynard Mack argued that 'we have been too
much concerned in this century with the verbal, which is only part of
the picture' and so he set out to explore what '*does* happen in a
Shakespeare tragedy' (p. 32; his italics). He noted the play's scenes of
madness and its many journeys, and asked whether Hamlet experi-
ences a 'recovery of sorts' before the final moments. One year later, in
The Story of the Night: Studies in Shakespeare's Major Tragedies, John
Holloway sought neither 'themes', 'values' or 'insights', nor a judgement on Hamlet. Instead, he asked what 'outstanding and momen-
tous experience' the tragedy gave to an audience. This he sought in
'the whole action, the whole developing course that [a tragedy]
pursues from the beginning of the work to the end'. In effect he studied the play as myth or ritual and was indebted to concurrent studies
of Greek tragedy and culture, anthropology, and psychology.
Hamlet's role:

> takes him from being the cynosure of his society to being estranged from
> it, and takes him, through a process of increasing alienation, to a point at
> which what happens to him suggests the expulsion of a scapegoat, or the
> sacrifice of a victim, or something of both.   (p. 135)

In *Hamlet versus Lear: Cultural Politics and Shakespeare's Art* (1993), R. A.
Foakes studied the changing fortunes of these two plays over the
greater part of the twentieth century. Having shown the close
connections between criticism of Shakespeare and current cultural
attitudes, he concluded that a scrupulous attention to words and

ideas was yielding to a concern for 'the whole play' and its effect on readers and viewers in Shakespeare's age and our own (p. 223). This new emphasis on the entire play looks back to studies of tragic form and theatrical traditions, as exemplified in Madeleine Doran's *Endeavors of Art* (1954) and M. C. Bradbrook's *Themes and Conventions of Elizabethan Tragedy* (1935), but interest in the play's effect on an audience or reader is a new element that called for experiential criticism and viewed the text in a lively and social context.

(iii)   Character

Granville Barker shared a long-standing concern with Hamlet's character with many other critics who were able to refine their thinking with a twentieth-century understanding of psychology. In *Shakespeare and Tragedy* (1981), John Bailey distinguished Shakespearean tragedy from Greek, French, Spanish and German tragedies because 'the mere fact and story of consciousness replaces both action and idea'. In other Elizabethan tragedies 'the avenger simplifies, feeling that one act will cure all', but 'for Hamlet his duty serves to reveal the infinite irreconcilable complications of living'. It is 'his consciousness that fills the play' and the critic's task is to understand those processes (pp. 6 and 176).

Ernest Jones's *Hamlet and Oedipus* (1900; revised edn 1949) was a highly influential study of psychoneurosis. Basing his view on the work of Freud and his successors and treating the character as a patient, Jones argued that Hamlet's early history ensured that:

> his uncle incorporates the deepest and most buried part of his own personality, so that he cannot kill him without also killing himself. . . . Only when he has . . . brought himself to the door of death is he free to fulfil his duty, to avenge his father, and to slay his other self – his uncle. (p. 100)

Later critics have elaborated this approach. For example, Janet Adelman's *Suffocating Mothers* (1992) is informed by twin interests in role-playing and fantasies of maternal origin. Hamlet's 'man and wife is one flesh' (IV.iii.54) provides a text for considering his 'confrontation with the maternal body':

> [Gertrude's] failure to serve her son as repository of his father's ideal image ... [and] her failure to differentiate between his father and his father's brother has put an intolerable strain on Hamlet by making him the only repository of his father's image. ...
>
> Ophelia becomes dangerous to Hamlet in so far as she becomes identified in his mind with the contaminating maternal body, the mother who has borne him.   (pp. 13–14)

Hamlet's recovery of his father's signet ring (V.ii.48–9) is seen as the means of repossessing the 'idealized father' (pp. 34–5).

In *Dream Works* (1987), Kay Stockholder gives a 'literary interpretation based on dream theory' that provides a similar diagnosis but with a different emphasis. She views the dreams of Shakespeare's protagonists as dreams taking place 'within the author's head' and, locating a 'core fantasy' in a play, notes the 'movements towards and away from it' (see pp. 12–16, and notes). Hamlet's dream 'hovers on the brink of nightmare' so that he tries to escape to Wittenberg: 'eroticized violence [tends] to alternate between male and female objects, and for their images to fuse'. The Ghost reappears:

> at the very moment [Hamlet] vents his most violent passions against Gertrude. ... By visualizing or imaginatively spying on a sexually active Claudius, Hamlet both denies and vicariously satisfies his desire for Gertrude. ... [Having brought] Hamlet as close to sexual satisfaction in life as he will come, these images disappear from the remainder of the play as Hamlet begins his progress towards the grave.   (pp. 58–9)

More temperate thoughts are also unsatisfied: he 'secretly condemns in Fortinbras the heroic virtues he overtly admires in his father, in Horatio secretly condones aspects of himself he overtly condemns' (pp. 42–3). For Shakespeare, the tragedy may well have been an expression of his own 'divided sexual impulse' and unsatisfied aspirations (pp. 240–1, n. 24).

(iv)   Context

Two World Wars and an increasingly politicized theatre have brought a wider view of the play and its effect in performance.

Writing in occupied Poland and taking his cue from Bertolt Brecht's *Little Organum for the Theatre*, Jan Kott gave a wake-up call in *Shakespeare our Contemporary* (translated in 1964). Instead of asking 'who Hamlet really was', he drew attention to four young persons:

> all involved in a bloody political and family drama. As a result, three of them will die; the fourth will, more or less by chance, become the king of Denmark. . . . None of them has chosen his part; it is imposed on them from outside; *Hamlet* is a drama of imposed situations.   (p. 56)

Traditional critics questioned many of Kott's assumptions but gradually the study of Shakespeare became politicized and found common ground with earlier critics who had sought to recreate an 'Elizabethan world picture'. But whereas B. L. Joseph's *Conscience and the King* (1953) or Fredson Bowers's *Elizabethan Revenge Tragedy* (1959) had sought to read the text in the light of generally received beliefs and moral judgements of Shakespeare's day, a new generation of scholars was concerned with how lives were lived, who possessed power, and who had to submit to others. Stephen Greenblatt's *Hamlet in Purgatory* (2001) addresses religious practices as well as the doctrines and sermons on which earlier studies had focused. Michael Bristol's examination of plebeian culture in *Carnival and Theater* (1985) leads to the conclusion that 'patterns of crowning and uncrowning, [and] of laughing at death, are perhaps more fully elaborated in *Hamlet* than in any other play (p. 185). Following studies of the place of travesty, devilry, the flouting of authority, and laugher in the social life of the audience for whom the play was written, Hamlet's taunting of Claudius after hiding Polonius's corpse and the comic banter of the clown–gravediggers are the texts on which this argument is based.

The play's reflection of real-life sexual and gender relations has been studied more closely than before. For example, Lisa Jardine's *Reading Shakespeare Historically* (1996) considers the plays from the view point of 'non-élite men and all women' and the 'events' in which they were caught up (p. 36). Catherine Belsey's *Shakespeare and the Loss of Eden* (1999) is based on visual as well as written evidence for marital violence and cruelty to children that co-existed with the admonitions of Elizabethan homilies and a desire for stable relationships. With regard to *Hamlet*, she shows how:

> Family values, the proper love of a son for his father, enmesh Hamlet in a web of anxiety, deceit, and death: tragedy stems from the commitment the family elicits. Both in Genesis and in Shakespeare, love and hate are inextricably entwined; and the greater the emotional investment, the greater the potential disruption of the security and stability. . . . The family, as a place of passion, is also, and correspondingly, the source of our greatest peril.   (pp. 173–4)

That Catherine Belsey should turn her attention, in conclusion, to 'our' predicament in today's society is typical of many critics writing today. On all sides, they acknowledge that we 'make' our own Shakespeare as we read and, in doing so, uncover unforeseen subtleties in the texts. For *Hamlet* this process started long ago – for example, 'we . . . are Hamlet' (p. 161, above) – because the text is full of uncertainties and speculations: about 'where truth is hid' and what is the nature of the Ghost or the 'heart of [Hamlet's] mystery'. The tragedy has engaged writers, artists and musicians in many divergent ways, as well as dramatists, novelists, poets, critics and scholars. A European view of the great wake of imaginative and intellectual activity that has followed the play in its passage down the years can be gained from Martin Scofield's *The Ghosts of Hamlet: The Play and Modern Writers* (1980). In the theatre, new interpretations occur with almost every production, each one influenced by the date of performance and the nature of the audience. Towards the end of the twentieth century, the number and variety of these reactions, creative, critical and theatrical, have been greatly extended through productions and study undertaken in almost every country in the world.

Further Reading

By no means a complete bibliography of *Hamlet*, this readers' guide gives details of books quoted in the course of this Handbook that will be found in larger libraries today, together with other relevant and recent books, accompanied by brief descriptions of their usefulness.

1 The Texts and Early Performances

(i) *Editions*

Editions of the play with a collation and annotations include the New Penguin, ed. T. J. B. Spencer (London: Penguin, 1980; revised editions, 1996, 2005); the Arden, ed. Harold Jenkins (London: Methuen, 1982); the Oxford Edition, ed. G. R. Hibbard (Oxford: Oxford University Press, 1987); the New Cambridge, ed. Philip Edwards (Cambridge: Cambridge University Press, 1985; updated edition, 2003). All these have been reprinted numerous times and give information and references regarding the known facts of the first printed texts and early performances.

The New Penguin edition is used for quotations and references to the play in this Handbook, but readers will find little difficulty in using any of the others or any recent edition of Shakespeare's *Complete Works*; only in prose passages is the lining liable to be very different.

(ii) *Theatre practice and theatre history*

Andrew Gurr, *The Shakespearean Stage, 1574–1642*, 3rd edition (Cambridge: Cambridge University Press, 1992), a thoroughly responsible account of what is known about the theatrical conditions in which Shakespeare's plays were first performed.

Peter Thomson, *Shakespeare's Theatre* (London: Routledge & Kegan Paul, 1983; 2nd edition, 1992); includes a chapter on '*Hamlet* and the actor'.

2   The Play's Sources and Cultural Context

(i)   Sources

Narrative and Dramatic Sources of Shakespeare, vol. vii, ed. Geoffrey Bullough (London: Routledge & Kegan Paul, and New York: Columbia University Press, 1973); reprints both a translation of *Historiae Danicae* and *The History of Hamblet*, together with a number of analogues and possible minor sources.

Kenneth Muir, *The Sources of Shakespeare's Plays* (London: Methuen, 1977), a careful discussion of probable and possible minor literary sources.

(ii)   Cultural context

Paul Griffiths, *Youth and Authority: Formative Experience in England, 1560–1640* (Oxford: Clarendon Press, 1996); although not concerned with royal families and practices, it is informative about the effects of the generation-gap that divides the characters in *Hamlet*.

Steven Mullaney, *The Place of the Stage* (Chicago: University of Chicago Press, 1988), an account of the cultural and topographical contexts of Elizabethan and Jacobean theatres.

Lawrence Stone, *The Family, Sex and Marriage in England, 1500–1800* (London: Weidenfeld & Nicolson, 1977), a study that illuminates developments in private life that relate to personal relationships in *Hamlet*.

Keith Thomas, *Religion and the Decline of Magic* (Oxford and New York: Oxford University Press, 1971), a seminal work dealing with superstition and belief in ghosts in the age of Shakespeare.

4   Key Productions and Performances

Ruby Cohn, *Modern Shakespeare Off-shoots* (Princeton, NJ: Princeton University Press, 1976); its longest chapter is on adaptations of *Hamlet*.

Anthony B. Dawson, *Hamlet*, Shakespeare in Performance series (Manchester: Manchester University Press, 1995), a stage history of the play with attention paid to the cultural background of productions; although very selective in its treatment of recent productions, it gives detailed accounts of two from 1980.

Rosamond Gilder, *John Gielgud's Hamlet* (London: Methuen, 1937); a scene by scene study of his performance and production as played in New York in the winter of 1936–7, with Gielgud's notes on 'The Hamlet Tradition'.

Hamlet Prince of Denmark, ed. Robert Hapgood, Shakespeare in Production series (Cambridge: Cambridge University Press, 1999); following an introductory stage history, the play text is reprinted with annotations that describe, line by line, how it has been spoken and staged in a large number of productions.

Alan Hughes, *Henry Irving, Shakespearean* (Cambridge: Cambridge University Press, 1981); a well-documented account of Irving's performance and production.

Andy Lavender, *Hamlet in Pieces: Shakespeare Reworked: Peter Brook, Robert Lepage, Robert Wilson* (London: Nick Hern Books, 2001); includes an account of Brook's subsequent production of the play.

Michael Pennington, *Hamlet, a User's Guide* (London: Nick Hern, 1996), an account of the play in performance by a recent actor of the role.

Marvin Rosenberg, *The Masks of Hamlet* (Berkeley, CA: University of California Press, 1992).

Richard L. Sterne, *John Gielgud Directs Richard Burton in Hamlet* (London: Heinemann, 1967), an actor's journal of rehearsals in preparation for an opening on Broadway in April 1964.

5   The Play on Screen

Deborah Cartmell, *Interpreting Shakespeare on Screen* (Basingstoke and London: Macmillan, 2000); includes a chapter on 'Critical and Filmic Representations of *Hamlet*'.

Diane E. Henderson (ed.), *A Concise Companion to Shakespeare on Screen* (Oxford: Blackwell, 2005); contains Robert Shaughnessy's 'Stage,

Screen and Nation: *Hamlet* and the Space of History', a thought-provoking account of *Hamlet* on screen.

Grigori Kozintsev, *Shakespeare: Time and Conscience*, trans. Joyce Vining (New York: Hill and Wang, 1996); contains an illuminating journal made while preparing and filming *Hamlet*.

(i)   Films referred to in this Handbook

Hamlet, 1948, Laurence Olivier as Hamlet, also directing; 155 minutes.
Hamlet, 1964, translated by Boris Pasternak; director Grigori Kozintsev, in Russian with English subtitles; 142 minutes.
Hamlet, 1969, director Tony Richardson; 112 minutes.
Hamlet, 1990, director Franco Zeffirelli; 129 minutes.
Hamlet, 1996, Kenneth Branagh as Hamlet, also directing; 232 minutes.
Hamlet, 2000, director Michael Almereyda; 123 minutes.

(ii)   Further readily available films and videos

Hamlet, 1980, director Rodney Bennett, Derek Jacobi as Hamlet, Claire Bloom as Gertrude; BBC TV Shakespeare; 215 minutes.
Hamlet, 1954, director John Gielgud, Richard Burton as Hamlet; video of New York performance; 90 minutes.

6   Critical Assessments

From the great number of books and articles currently or recently available, the following are those quoted or referred to in Chapter 6.

Janet Adelman, *Suffocating Mothers: Fantasies of Maternal Origin in Shakespeare's Plays, 'Hamlet' to 'The Tempest'* (New York and London: Routledge, 1992).
John Bailey, *Shakespeare and Tragedy* (London, Boston and Henley: Routledge & Kegan Paul, 1981).
Harley Granville Barker, *Prefaces to Shakespeare, third series: 'Hamlet'* (London: Sidgwick & Jackson, 1937; and many times reprinted by other publishers).

Catherine Belsey, *Shakespeare and the Loss of Eden: The Construction of Family Values in Early Modern Culture* (Basingstoke: Macmillan, 1999).

Fredson Bowers, *Elizabethan Revenge Tragedy, 1587–1642* (Gloucester, MA: Peter Smith, 1959).

M. C. Bradbrook, *Themes and Conventions of Elizabethan Tragedy* (Cambridge: Cambridge University Press, 1935).

A C. Bradley, *Shakespearean Tragedy: Lectures on 'Hamlet', 'Othello', 'King Lear', 'Macbeth'* (London: Macmillan, 1904; and many times reprinted).

Bertolt Brecht, *Little Organum for the Theatre*, trans. in John Willett (tr.), *Brecht on Theatre* (London: Methuen, 1964).

Michael D. Bristol, *Carnival and Theater: Plebeian Culture and the Structure of Authority in Renaissance England* (New York and London: Methuen, 1985).

Madeleine Doran, *Endeavors of Art: A Study of Form in Elizabethan Drama* (Madison: University of Wisconsin Press, 1954).

R. A. Foakes, *Hamlet versus Lear: Cultural Politics and Shakespeare's Art* (Cambridge: Cambridge University Press, 1993).

Michael Goldman, *Acting and Action in Shakespearean Tragedy* (Princeton, NJ: Princeton University Press, 1985).

Stephen J. Greenblatt, *Hamlet in Purgatory* (Princeton, NJ: Princeton University Press, 2001).

John Holloway, *The Story of the Night: Studies in Shakespeare's Major Tragedies* (London: Routledge & Kegan Paul, 1961).

E. A. J. Honigmann, *Shakespeare: Seven Tragedies: The Dramatist's Manipulation of Response* (London and Basingstoke: Macmillan, 1976; republished as *Seven Tragedies Revisited*).

Lisa Jardine, *Reading Shakespeare Historically* (London and New York: Routledge, 1996).

Ernest Jones, *Hamlet and Oedipus* (London: Gollancz, 1949).

B. L. Joseph, *Conscience and the King: A Study of 'Hamlet'* (London: Chatto & Windus, 1953).

G. Wilson Knight, *The Shakespearian Tempest* (London: Methuen, 1932).

L. C. Knights, *'Hamlet' and other Shakespearean Essays* (Cambridge: Cambridge University Press, 1979).

Jan Kott, *Shakespeare Our Contemporary*, trans. Boleslaw Taborski (London: Methuen, 1964).

Michael Long, *The Unnatural Scene: A Study in Shakespearean Tragedy* (London: Methuen, 1976).

Maynard Mack, 'The Jacobean Shakespeare', *Jacobean Theatre*, ed. John Russell Brown and Bernard Harris (London: Edward Arnold, 1960).

M. M. Mahood, *Shakespeare's Wordplay* (London: Methuen, 1957).

Norman Rabkin, *Shakespeare and the Problem of Meaning* (Chicago: Chicago University PRess, 1981).

Martin Scofield, *The Ghosts of Hamlet: The Play and Modern Writers* (Cambridge: Cambridge University Press, 1980).

D. A. Stauffer, *Shakespeare's World of Images: The Development of his Moral Ideas* (New York: W. W. Norton, 1969).

Kay Stockholder, *Dream Works: Lovers and Families in Shakespeare's Plays* (Toronto and London: University of Toronto Press, 1987).

Caroline Spurgeon, *Shakespeare's Imagery and What it Tells Us* (Cambridge: Cambridge University Press, 1935; and many times reprinted).

Index

Act division, 49–50, 97
actors, acting, 10, 20–2, 133
  boy actors, 104
Adelman, Janet, *Suffocating Mothers*, 166–7
Agate, James, 142
Almereyda, Michael, 159
Archer, William, 140
  The Fashionable Tragedian, 136
Arden of Faversham (anon.), 13
Armin, Robert, 26

Bailey, John, *Shakespeare and Tragedy*, 166
Beckett, Samuel, *Waiting for Godot*, 154
Belleforest, François de, *Histoires tragiques*, 13, 15–17
Belsey, Catherine, *Shakespeare and the Loss of Eden*, 168–9
Bergman, Ingmar, 152
Betterton, Thomas, 134
Bible, the, 17, 38, 50, 67, 94, 114, 121, 125–6, 169
Bonham-Carter, Helena, 158
Book of Common Prayer, the, 29
Booth, Edwin, 135–6
Boswell, Lawrence, 152
Bowers, Fredson, *Elizabethan Revenge Tragedy*, 168

Bradbrook, M. C., *Themes and Conventions*, 165
Bradley, A. C., *Shakespearean Tragedy*, 162, 163
Branagh, Kenneth, 158
Brecht, Bertolt, *Little Organum*, 168
Bright, Timothy, *Treatise of Melancholy*, 18
Bristol, Michael, *Carnival and Theatre*, 168
Brook, Peter, 154
Bryden, Ronald, 148
Burbage, Richard, 4, 119
Burton, Richard, 145–6
Bury, John, 148–9

Calvin, John, 125
Chamberlain's Men, 2, 9, 10, 12, 22
Chapman, George, 19
Christianity, reference to, 17, 29–30, 31, 34, 35, 36, 38, 48, 50, 51, 54, 88–9, 93, 94, 110 113, 120, 125–6, 130–1, 168
Ciulei, Liviu, 153
Close, Glenn, 158
clowns, 26–7, 54, 112–18, 122–3, 168
Cohn, Ruby, *Modern Shakespeare Off-shoots*, 153–4
Coleridge, Samuel, 161
Condell, Henry, 6

costumes, 10, 35, 46–7, 82, 93, 118, 123, 135, 145, 147, 149, 152
Court, the, 22–6
Craig, Edward Gordon, 140, 144

Daniels, Ron, 151
Darlington, W. A., 141
Devereux, Robert, Earl of Essex, 9, 17–18
Disher, M. Willson, 142
Donne, John, 19
  Satires, 24–5
Doran, Madeleine, *Endeavors of Art*, 166
Dowden, Edward, *Shakespere: . . . his Mind and Art*, 161–2

Elizabeth I, 22, 23, 87, 156
Evelyn, John, 160
Eyre, Richard, 151

Farquhar, George, *Discourse on Comedy*, 160
Feingold, Michael, 153
film scripts, 156–9
Florio, John, 18–19
Foakes, R. A., '*Hamlet*' versus '*Lear*', 165–6
Folio, the First, 3, 5–8, 49–50, 71, 74, 80–2, 86, 90, 99, 101, 103–5, 113, 114, 118–19, 120, 128, 130, 132, 152
  cuts in, 6–8, 33, 101, 111, 124, 125, 126
  rewriting, evidence of, 7–8, 74, 101, 130
Freud, Sigmund, 144, 166

Garrick, David, 48, 134
ghosts, 12–13, 17, 18, 33

Gibson, Mel, 157–8
Gielgud, John, 140–6
Gilder, Rosamond, *John Gielgud's Hamlet*, 142–4
Globe Theatre, London, 9
Goethe, Johann Wolfgang von, *Wilhelm Meister's Apprenticeship*, 160–1
Goldman, Michael, *Acting and Action*, 164
Granville Barker, Harley, *Preface to 'Hamlet'*, 164–5, 166
Greek tragedy, 165, 166
Greenblatt, Stephen, *Hamlet in Purgatory*, 168
Greene, Robert, 12

Hall, Peter, 146–9, 152
hallucination, 93
Hamblet, History of, 13–17, 58
Hapgood, Robert, '*Hamlet*' in *Performance*, 164
Harvey, Gabriel, 9
Hazlitt, William, *Characters of Shakespeare's Plays*, 135, 161
Hemings, John, 6
Holloway, John, *Story of the Night*, 165
Honigmann, Ernst, *Stability of Shakespeare's Text*, 3
  Seven Tragedies, 164
Hughes, Alan, *Henry Irving, Shakespearean*, 136–40

Ibsen, Henrik, 136
Irace, Kathleen O. (ed.), *Hamlet*, First Quarto, 3
Irving, Henry, 48, 136–40

James I, 26
Jardine, Lisa, *Reading Shakespeare Historically*, 168

Johnson, Samuel (ed.), *Shakespeare's
    Works*, 160
Jones, Ernest, *Hamlet and Oedipus*,
    166
Jonson, Ben, 19
Joseph, B. L., *Conscience and the King*,
    168

Kean, Edmund, 135, 137, 161
Keats, John, 135
Kemble, John Philip, 135, 137, 161
Kingsley, Ben, 150
King's Men, 2, 6, 10
Kline, Kevin, 153
Kott, Jan, *Shakespeare Our
    Contemporary*, 168
Knights, L.C., '*Hamlet*' and . . . *Essays*,
    163, 164
Kozintsev, Grigori, 155–6, 157
Kyd, Thomas, *Spanish Tragedy*, 5, 13,
    17, 18, 20

Lavater, Ludwig, *Of Ghosts and
    Spirits*, 18
Lavender, Andy, *Hamlet in Pieces*,
    154
Lepage, Robert, 154
Livings, Henry, *Eh?*, 148
Lodge, Thomas, *Wit's Misery*, 12–13
London, 26–7, 28, 66
Long, Michael, *Unnatural Scene*, 164
Luther, Martin, 17
Lyceum Theatre, London, 136,
    139–40
Lyubimov, Yuri, 151

Machiavelli, Niccolò, 112
    The Prince, 59–60
Mack, Maynard, 'The Jacobean
    Shakespeare', 165

Macready, William Charles, 135
Mahood, M. M., *Shakespeare's
    Wordplay*, 163
Marlowe, Christopher, 11, 19, 69
    Dr Faustus, 17, 30, 63
Marston, John (critic), *Our Recent
    Actors*, 135
Marston, John (playwright),
    Antonio's Revenge, 11
McDonald, Antony, 151
Mielziner, Jo, 144
Montaigne, Michel de, *Essays*, 18–19,
    65, 126
morality plays, 116
Motley (designers), 144
Muir, Kenneth, *Shakespeare's Sources*,
    18
Müller, Heiner, *The Hamlet Machine*,
    199

Nashe, Thomas, 12,
    Pierce Penniless, 18
National Theatre, London, 152
New Theatre, London, l40

Old Vic Theatre, London, 140, 141
Olivier, Laurence, 157
Orange Tree, The, London, 150

Pasternak, Boris, 152
properties, stage, 10, 62, 75, 86,
    90, 92, 102, 109, 110, 113, 114,
    116–18, 121, 123–4, 126–8, 131,
    134, 149
prose, 16, 57, 63, 64, 74–5, 78, 98,
    100, 109, 113
Pryce, Jonathan, 150–1
Public Theatre, New York, 153
punctuation, 5–6, 50, 51
Pushkin Theatre, Leningrad, 155

Quarto, First, 1–5, 56, 62, 81–2, 88,
    90, 93, 99, 104, 109, 113, 118–18,
    120, 128, 130, 150
Quarto, Second, 2–8, 71, 74, 82, 86,
    91, 98, 101–12, 103, 104, 105, 109,
    111, 113, 126, 128, 130, 152
Queen's Theatre, London, 141

Rabkin, Norman, *Problem of
    Meaning*, 163
Raleigh, Sir Walter, 19
Rhys, Paul, 152–3
religion, *see* Christianity
Rich, Frank, 153
Richardson, Tony, 157
Robin Hood, 29
Rome, ancient, 31, 33
Rosenberg, Marvin, *Masks of Hamlet*,
    164
Roundhouse, London, 157
Rowe, Nicholas, *Life of Shakespeare*,
    134
Royal Court Theatre, London, 150
Royal Shakespeare Company (RSC),
    146–9, 150
Russell, Edward R., *Irving as Hamlet*,
    136–40
Rylance, Mark, 151

Saxo Grammaticus, 13, 15
Scofield, Martin, *Ghosts of Hamlet*,
    169
Seneca, 12–13, 17, 18, 126
Shakespeare, William
    As You Like It, 26, 29, 66, 124
    Henry IV, 147
    Henry V, 16–17, 18, 50, 147
    Henry VI, 148
    Julius Caesar, 9, 12, 16, 17, 39, 67
    King Lear, 19, 34, 67

Love's Labour's Lost, 10, 115, 124
Lucrece, Rape of, 9
Macbeth, 84, 126
Merchant of Venice, 130
Midsummer Night's Dream, 16, 148,
    164
Much Ado about Nothing, 157
Richard II, 54, 106, 130
Romeo and Juliet, 4, 12, 124, 138, 157
Tempest, The, 19
Twelfth Night, 26
Venus and Adonis, 9
Shaw, George Bernard, 136
Sidney, Sir Philip, 19
Smoktunovsky, Innokenti, 156, 157
Spencer, T.J.B. (ed.), *Hamlet*
    (Penguin), 7
Spenser, Edmund, 19
Spurgeon, Caroline, *Shakespeare's
    Imagery*, 163
Stationers' Register, The, 2, 9, 19
Stauffer, D. A., *Shakespeare's World of
    Images*, 163
Steele, Richard, *The Tatler*, 134
Sterne, Richard L., *John Gielgud
    Directs Burton*, 145–6
Stockholder, Kay, *Dream Works*,
    167
Stoppard, Tom, *Rosencrantz and
    Guildenstern are Dead*, 154
Stormare, Peter, 152
Stratford-upon-Avon, 28, 146, 150,
    151

Taganka Theatre, Moscow, 151
Terry, Ellen, 138–9, 140
texts, production, 139, 151, 152,
    153–4
Theatre, The, London, 9, 12–13
trapdoor, 34, 51

Ur-Hamlet, 12, 13, 17, 33

Virgil, 69
Vysotsky, Vladimir, 151–2

Walters, Sam, 150
Warner, David, 146–9
Webster, John, 19
  Duchess of Malfi, 26
Williamson, Nichol, 157
Wilson, Robert, 154

Wilson Knight, G., *The Shakespearian
    Tempest*, 163
Winter, William, *Edwin Booth*,
    135–6
Wriothesley, Henry, Earl of
    Southampton, 17–19

Young, B. A., 150
Young Vic Theatre, London, 152

Zeffirelli, Franco, 157–8, 159